*To the memory
of the baby who has died.*

iv.

CONTENTS

CHAPTER 13 - THE PHYSICIAN'S RESPONSE

CHAPTER 14 - THE ROLE OF THE FUNERAL DIRECTOR

CHAPTER 15 - THE ROLE OF THE CLERGY

CHECKLISTS
ONE-TO-ONE HELPER

FOREWORD

In June 1978, when my first child died during birth, health professionals and hospital staffs were mostly unprepared for dealing with such a loss. Some staff members were sympathetic and helpful; others said foolish and hurtful things or acted as if nothing had happened. Over the following few months, I discovered that many others like me had also experienced losses in pregnancy and had grieved intensely for those babies with very little understanding from those around us.

I am very glad to be able to say that many things have changed since 1978. My own experience and that of my good friend Susan Borg several months later led us to write *When Pregnancy Fails* because we felt that there had been no book for us to turn to. There are now many books, and a great deal of effort has been made in the past few years to educate and prepare hospital staff to know what to do to help families so that their tragedies may be a little bit less painful.

The credit for these changes goes to some caring professionals and to parents who responded to their tragedies by writing, organizing, sharing, and working for change. The work of some very special nurses and physicians as well as dedicated parents has resulted in major changes in hospital policy and in the formation over the last few years of hundreds of support programs for families who have suffered a miscarriage, an ectopic pregnancy, a stillbirth, or the death of an infant. Both kinds of efforts are needed. Families need attention and need to know that they have some choices in the immediate period following the loss. But they also need support through the months that follow, since grieving is something that does not go away in a few days or weeks. Therefore the support programs and other kinds of follow-up measures can help families know that if they are still hurting a year later, they are not unusual or crazy, and others will be there to listen and to care about their pain.

When Susan Borg and I were doing the research for *When Pregnancy*

Fails, we found that almost two-thirds of the individuals whom we interviewed expressed dissatisfaction with some aspect of the care they had received from their physicians and from the hospital staff. Most felt very alone in their grief, with few people to turn to for support. Much of this was due to lack of understanding, to the uncomfortableness which is felt when a death occurs, and to the lack of options available for families. As a result of the work that has been done over the last few years and the publication of books like this one, parents who are now suffering loss in pregnancy should be less likely to find that the grief and pain over their bereavement is made worse by inadequate professional care and by isolation from others who share their feelings.

Resolve Through Sharing has been in the forefront of these efforts, and I congratulate them for bringing together the materials here. I trust that this book will provide comfort to people who are grieving for their babies and insights to those who seek to help them.

JUDITH N. LASKER

ACKNOWLEDGMENTS

The authors gratefully acknowledge . . .

Carolyn Smiley and Kathryn Goettl for their courage, commitment, and care in responding to the needs of bereaved parents. It is their practice which became the basis and impetus for the *Resolve Through Sharing* program.

Resolve Through Sharing parents and counselors throughout the U.S.A., Canada, and the Philippines for their openness in sharing their experiences and feelings. Their heartache, concern, and willingness to reach out to others have helped us to understand their needs. We are forever changed.

The bereaved parents and health care professionals who reviewed our manuscript and offered suggestions, advice, and encouragement. Especially Glen Davidson, Ph.D., whose sensitivity fine tuned aspects of the book.

Pam Padesky, Adrian Roberg, Mark Thompson, Barbara Possin, Luanne Sorenson, Julie MacDonald, Ted Peck, J. Michael Hartigan, and Donna Proudfit for their vision in believing that this could and should be done; Donald Smith and Jacqueline Siefkas for their support and understanding during this project; Gracia Sandager for her many hours of typing and photocopying.

La Crosse Lutheran Hospital/Gundersen Clinic, Ltd. for supporting the program and responding to the needs of health care professionals and bereaved parents across the nation.

Lutheran Hospital Foundation, Inc., and Nora A. Starcher, CFRE, Executive Director, without whose financial support this dream could not have become a reality.

Margaret Larson, our editor, whose sensitivity and understanding strengthened our book.

Mary Abel, whose creativity and words of encouragement we could not do without.

— and —

Sister Jane Marie Lamb, our inspiration. Her wisdom and guidance shine as a beacon for us all.

xii.

INTRODUCTION

When most of us hear of a pregnancy, whether it is ours or another's, we think of a Gerber baby, fresh from a bath, smelling of powder and lotion, and wrapped in a terry cloth towel. We think of the child celebrating at a first birthday party, going to kindergarten, and playing dress-up or Little League. We wonder if the child will have his mother's nose or her father's curly hair.

Dreams and images are part of every pregnancy, but not every dream comes true. More often than most of us ever imagine, pregnancies do not always end happily ever after.

Each year, over half a million dreams are shattered. Out of 3.3 million babies born alive, some 30,000 die during the first 28 days. Another 33,000 babies are stillborn. Miscarriage occurs in 15 to 20 percent of pregnancies, while ectopic pregnancy occurs in one percent.

It is little comfort to grieving parents that infant mortality is much less than what it was at the turn of the century when one out of ten babies died. Parents cannot cuddle statistics. All that matters to a parent whose baby has died is that infant was their child.

It is hard for persons who have never experienced a loss to realize just how dismal these parents find their world. With shattering suddenness young persons who generally have never experienced death must face an intense and often unexpected loss.

This agonizing grief has been little understood until recently. Often, the ones parents rely on most — relatives, friends and acquaintances — are unable to give the support bereaved parents need. They do not understand the loss and the grief because in the eyes of society the child has not "lived." They may not recognize relationships between parents and baby begin early in pregnancy and, many times, before conception.

To mothers and fathers, the baby was very much alive regardless of how long he or she lived. They were parents even if the child did not live outside the womb. "I am still a parent," one angry father said. "I have a need for someone from society to say that I am a parent. Many, many people forget that. That is one of the hardest things that I have to deal with."

Grief cannot be compared, measured, or quantified. Parents do not mourn for a child according to how long they "knew" him or her. The death of a baby is mourned, quite simply, because parents have lost their future. They have lost their hopes and dreams for that child and their life with her.

There are several reasons why parents may not get the support they need. The average family moves every three to five years. We no longer live next door to the same families for years. Our society is not only more mobile but our relationships also are shorter in duration.

While mother and grandmother might have provided support in years past, today they may be separated from the grieving parents by hundreds of miles. It is ironic that today the slogan "Reach Out and Touch Someone" refers to a long-distance call, rather than a personal visit or a warm, sympathetic hug.

When A Baby Dies: A Handbook for Healing and Helping is written because so many grieving parents must receive their hugs from friends, counselors, clergy, or health professionals. These persons, particularly if they haven't experienced the loss of a baby, may not understand the emotions that occur at a time like this. Yet they must help parents realize their feelings following their baby's death are normal and that there are no thoughts or emotions others haven't had.

By offering When A Baby Dies: A Handbook for Healing and Helping, we do not suggest that the pain parents feel can magically be "healed" by this book. The life of a parent who has lost a child will never return to what it was before that baby died.

Healing, to us, does not mean a quick cure; healing is putting the loss in perspective. Parents will not get there overnight or by reading this book. Grieving takes time - lots of it.

One of the difficulties in a loss of any kind is that, even beyond the immediate pain, there is a change in those who experience it. Forever more, parents feel a vulnerability to all the perils in life. Losing a loved one is no longer an abstract thought. A bad thing has happened to good people. It happened to them. They fear it or other sad events can occur in their lives again.

Still there is a positive side to a loss, which we call the "new normal." Parents' lives are changed forever, but many report when they are back to "normal" they have a new sense of awareness and sensitivity to those around them. They also have a greater appreciation for life, family, and friends.

Many even report that with this "new normal" comes greater self-esteem. Once they might have looked at others in crisis and thought "I could never live through that." Now, they recognize their own inner strength and ability to go on after a personal crisis.

Resolve Through Sharing is a comprehensive, hospital-based, perinatal bereavement program for families experiencing miscarriage, ectopic pregnancy, stillbirth, and newborn death. It is designed to ensure that consistent, sensitive care is given to each and every grieving parent and family from the moment the baby dies, through the period of grieving, and for as long as the family desires. The program began in 1981 at La Crosse Lutheran Hospital/Gundersen Clinic, Ltd., in La Crosse, Wisconsin. Since becoming national in scope, thousands of families are touched each year by our hospital-based *Resolve Through Sharing* programs and *Resolve Through Sharing* counselors. In addition, educational and certification programs, lectures, and publications are presented throughout the country.

We are sharing what we have learned because we believe that, for too long, the death of a baby through miscarriage, ectopic pregnancy, stillbirth, and newborn death has been dismissed as minor. To the loving parents, the baby was very real, very much alive, and continues to be a part of their lives.

HOW TO USE THIS BOOK

You might have this book in your hands because you and your partner have just experienced the loss of a pregnancy or the death of your newly-born infant. Or perhaps this occurred months or years ago and you still are trying to come to grips with the death of your baby. You might be reading this book because you are the grandparent or family friend of the baby who died. Or you might be a health professional, a funeral director, or a member of the clergy who is looking for ways to help a bereaved family.

This book was written for all of you.

The chapters entitled "Grief" and "Saying Good-Bye" offer general information and suggestions for anyone affected by a loss — whether they be the parents or those who are called upon to help the parents.

The other chapters contain specific information and suggestions.

We encourage you to read "Grief" and "Saying Good-Bye" and then go on to read the chapters that apply to you.

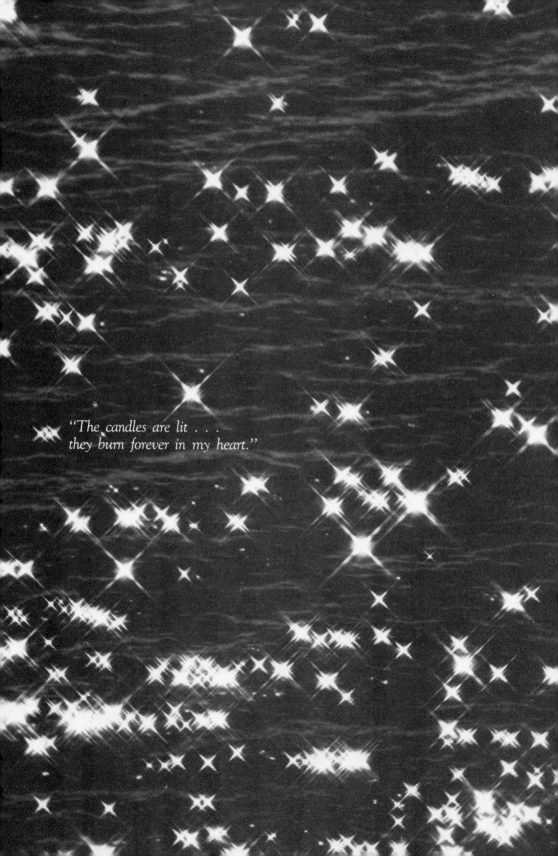

*"The candles are lit . . .
they burn forever in my heart."*

To Jessica

The candles are lit,
   but no song will be sung.
No laughter, no glee, of my little one
   who would have been three.

If you only knew the plans that would be
   made by your dad and me.
The cake to be baked . . .
The presents wrapped . . .
   and all the funny party hats.

The pictures taken by your dad, .
   of course,
As loving friends fill the house.

All of this is not meant to be,
since you were taken away from me.
   No birthday cake . . .
   No presents unwrapped . . .
   No pictures of you in your party hat.

But the candles are lit,
   Never to go out.
For they burn forever in my heart.

                              Love,
                              Mom

KATHIE MAYO

CHAPTER 1

*"All our dreams had come true
except he was dead . . ."*

GRIEF

REMEMBERING LUCAS

*T*im and Lori's dream family was two boys, close in age, running through their backyard. "Nicholas always would be ahead," Lori said. "A little boy would be following him."

The couple's dream nearly became reality. But their second son, Lucas, was stillborn. "All our dreams had come true except he was dead," his mother said sadly. Added his father, "That was the killer. He was a boy."

The first trouble came as Lori was in the labor and delivery unit at her community hospital. A doctor attempted to listen to the baby's heartbeat. "He kept going around and around and around my stomach. After about 15 minutes, he started getting really nervous, so I asked him, 'You hear a heartbeat, don't you?' I knew he would say everything was OK," Lori recalled. "But, he said, 'No I don't.' Then I got really upset."

The doctor, whom the couple described as "very caring," was extremely upset. "I don't know if it was his first loss or what," Tim said.

Lucas looked perfectly normal. His father said, "Even when we went through the delivery and the baby came out and the doctor said he was a boy, he looked just like Nick only he looked like he was sleeping."

Lori and Tim had tremendous support from family and friends following Lucas' death. Nearly all the workers at the company where they work attended the funeral. One co-worker gave them a hand-knit blanket which they wrapped around the baby in the casket. "We wanted him buried in that because it was made just for him and looked warm," Lori said. "It was the only thing we had that was totally Lucas."

Tim also gave the baby a gift. At the last minute, he took off a ring and put it in Lucas' casket. "I needed to give him something."

The family received a particularly touching card from the class of Tim's daughter, Jennifer, eleven-and-a-half. One class member, whose mother had experienced a miscarriage several months before, wrote, "I know what it feels like."

Nicholas, two-and-a-half, naturally did not understand why his brother died and said repeatedly, "No die. No die." He often asks to go to the cemetery, saying "I want to see Luke. I want to see Luke."

Despite tremendous support, it was difficult for Lori to handle Nicholas after she lost Lucas. "I was really nasty with Nicholas. He couldn't do anything right. I knew he was two-and-a-half years old but I wanted him to hug me and love me as a little baby."

A year after her loss, Lori became pregnant again. Her joy in the pregnancy was tempered with anger. Had Lucas lived, she would not have had to go through another pregnancy. "My body doesn't like to be pregnant," she said.

MENDING A BROKEN HEART

Before going through it, most of us think of grief as the immediate reaction we have to the loss of a loved one. To some it may be tears, while to others it may be the scream that comes from somewhere inside us when we learn that someone we love has died. Others think it is the numbness or shock that follows terrible news.

Grief is much, much more than that. It has been called the toughest job one ever has to do. It also has been described as nature's way of healing a broken heart.

Loss of a baby is a grief unprepared for and a grief least understood. It comes when most parents have had little or no experience with death.

Mourning is the natural way of adjusting to the loss. It is necessary and healthy for parents to express their feelings, no matter what they are.

While parents may carry elements of grief throughout their lives, the pain immediately following a loss is the most intense and deep. As one parent put it, "My emotions have never been on such a wild roller coaster. One hour I feel like we are going to make it through this and be so much closer, and then some little thing happens and my heart aches so badly for a baby I can hardly bear it."

Mourning is an individual matter, yet there are four common phases that have been described by John Bowlby and C. Murray Parkes. In grief, one moves among:

1) shock and numbness

2) searching and yearning

3) disorientation

4) reorganization.

The phases are not as clearly defined as they appear. Healing has bits and pieces of each phase, some say it has stops and starts. Parents describe these phases as coming in waves, with good and bad days washing over them. Parents are changed with each wave, never completely going back to what they were before.

Even in the beginning, the four phases may be felt all at the same time, or one may dominate. Parents may find their sadness triggered by seemingly small things such as a diaper commercial, baby food in the grocery store, or seeing a pregnant woman.

Healing is a journey at a snail's pace. A loss can strain all members of the family for 18 to 24 months or longer. Because healing might occur so slowly, some feel they are not moving at all. This is not the time for major decisions, such as changing jobs, changing relationships, or moving.

SHOCK AND NUMBNESS

The first news of a loss causes shock. Parents may be stunned one minute; angry, panicked, or distressed the next.

"My miscarriage happened so fast (less than four hours) without any time to contemplate what was going on," described one mother, "that I think I am still in shock and will have much to face as time passes."

Parents find it difficult to make decisions and to concentrate. They may feel it all is a dream and not really happening to them. Sometimes they may cry uncontrollably, while at other times they may sit and stare into space. This stunned disbelief is the way they cope with a shock that is too much to deal with all at once.

Still another common reaction for parents is being manic. They may laugh, or look and act as if they are on the top of the world. Some people may see them as the superwoman or superman, while others may be disconcerted by that response, believing the parents are just covering up their feelings.

SEARCHING AND YEARNING

During this phase, parents search for their baby because sometimes the child still seems very much alive. The struggle between the conscious and the unconscious to accept the reality of the baby's death causes bizarre thoughts and feelings. Some parents have even thought about kidnapping another baby. Some mothers fear they are losing their minds because they hear crying in the middle of the night, feel the baby kick, dream about the baby and being pregnant again, or just feel pregnant.

Mothers may be depressed that their body acts as though they still have a baby. "It just doesn't seem fair," one mother said. "I don't have a baby, but my body says I do." These normal reactions occur because the woman's body was preparing itself to care for a baby. After a loss, it takes time to adjust both physically and emotionally.

Emotional outbursts are common at this time. Anger may be directed at their partner, doctor, nurse, God, themselves, or even the baby.

Mothers, particularly, find themselves crying a lot. They may lose weight because they are nauseated or unable to eat. Or, they may eat a lot and gain weight. Mothers may be unable to sleep or may want to sleep all the time. They may experience restlessness and inability to concentrate. These reactions are caused, in part, by the high level of adrenalin in the body at the time of loss.

Going out in public or back to work may be especially hard for mothers who cannot bear to look at other pregnant women or to see babies. Some feel pain when they see a pregnant friend or hear a new baby cry. "A close friend of mine is pregnant," a mother with a recent loss said. "Her due date and mine were close to the same time. That hurts. I think about our kids growing up together, going to school together, like she and I did. I find myself staying away from her, not wanting to see her belly grow while mine stays flat and lifeless."

Some mothers yearn so much for their baby at this time that their arms ache. They may find themselves cradling or stroking some object of similar size and weight to that of the baby such as a cat, a rolling pin, or a beef roast. "I had nightmares about not holding her - the empty arms thing," a mother recalled. "My arms just hurt. If felt like I was walking around with two 20-pound weights."

Returning to work can be even more difficult for fathers, who are expected to be back to "business as usual," often the next day. Fathers are rarely asked how they are doing. Men also expect themselves to be "tough" and to work because someone has to continue earning an income.

Men's needs after a loss differ in other ways as well. Research conducted by Steven Merrill, a *Resolve Through Sharing* counselor, has shown that fathers often seek detailed information about the cause of the loss, whether it is likely to occur again, and how they can help their partners. "I had to know why this happened and what I could do to keep my wife from hurting so," a father said.

Parents, who find it difficult to answer questions about their pregnancy and baby, might entrust a friend to explain to others what happened. They also may need help from family and friends in caring for other children, for cleaning, shopping, and other errands.

Parents may find comfort in mementos from their baby. Recording their thoughts and feelings in a diary, journal, or on tape may be useful. Their thoughts become a resource to help them work out their feelings. Others may find reading books or articles about similar losses helpful.

After about two weeks, friends and family often call less frequently. At this time, and in the next few months, some parents find it useful to attend meetings of support groups for parents who have lost a baby through miscarriage, etcopic pregnancy, stillbirth, or newborn death.

"I needed someone to listen until I got through my 'endless talking' stage," explained a mother who attended a *Resolve Through Sharing* Parent Support Group meeting. "Being surrounded by other parents made me feel as if they really understood and that they valued whatever I wanted to share."

Many parents spend time looking for the reason their baby died. Their search may preoccupy much of their time and thoughts. "No one can give you a logical answer. You are told that it just happens and you are supposed to accept the face value of that fact," a father said. "But there is some reason and that why, or what, hangs on for always, unanswered. I wanted answers that no one could give me."

Many parents feel guilty. They constantly replay the event looking for cause within them for the death. One mother said it took her a long time before she could stop blaming herself. She believes other parents need to be reassured that they did not cause the death. "It is not because you got up in the morning and drank Diet Pepsi or coffee. It is not because when you filled the gas tank, you didn't turn your head to avoid the fumes. It wasn't anything you did. It is one of those things you can't explain."

When parents blame themselves they lose self-esteem. Some mothers feel they failed in "what they as a woman were supposed to do - have a baby."

Often, parents worry they are crying too much or, if they start, they won't be able to stop. They should be encouraged to express their feelings, not hide them. Tears shed during grief have more toxins than do regular tears. Tears actually can be healing.

"I still cry, but it's not the crying that is bothersome," a mother said months after her baby died. "It's the fact that I have no control over when I cry, how long, or with whom."

Still other emotions may bombard parents after a loss. They may wish they were dead instead of their baby or they may be angry at their baby for causing such suffering. Thoughts of suicide are not uncommon. Parents often express these thoughts by saying, "I'd be better off with my baby."

Anger and irritability may seem uncontrollable. Parents may find themselves short tempered, just because their emotions need to spill out somehow.

It is during this time - usually about four months after the loss - that parents need a routine physical exam for themselves. This is a time many families feel physically and emotionally exhausted. The natural disease-fighting mechanism is depressed in the body, making it more prone to illness and disease. An examination can pick up problems early, perhaps before they have a chance to become serious.

Parents also need to limit use of anti-depressant medicines or sleeping pills because the medications may delay expression of emotions or make parents more depressed. Sleeping pills should be taken every other or every third night and only for a limited period of time.

DISORIENTATION

After working through the powerful emotions in the Searching and Yearning phase, parents often have a time when they feel empty, lifeless, and hopeless. They have no interest in things they used to enjoy. They neglect their personal appearance and daily tasks. Attacks of anxiety are common, and parents often report feeling vulnerable, afraid other bad things might happen to them.

They may lack energy and feel they cannot get anything done. Often, they are more susceptible to flu, colds, and other illnesses.

This phase is difficult because it comes just when many people think they should be "over it." Family, friends and even parents themselves think they should be through with grief. Some parents feel bad about feeling bad. They may feel multiple losses - of pride, control, strength, and self-esteem. It is not uncommon for parents to wish they were dead, simply because their grief seems unbearable.

"I remember thinking I will never feel any better," a mother said. "That caused me a lot of problems. I thought there was something wrong with me."

Parents begin wondering if they are normal or going crazy. "You really start to doubt your sanity and wonder if you are going to live this way the rest of your life," another mother explained.

This is a time when couples often become very unhappy with each other, perhaps because they grieve in different ways. The parents need to encourage each other to be open about their feelings and to be sensitive to each other.

Exercise and activity also can provide relief from persistent thoughts of unhappiness.

It is during this phase that a friend or counselor can be particularly helpful to many parents. Parents may wonder if they are grieving normally, if they need to see a counselor. The checklist on page 11 may help parents understand their responses.

REORGANIZATION

Parents are often surprised when they experience signs of reorganization, of getting on with living again, of feeling "normal" again.

One mother's laugh startled her children one day. Worrying that something bad had happened, they ran into her room and found that, for the first time since their baby brother died, she had a moment of happiness.

These moments may come very early after a loss, or much later. They may worry parents who are concerned that if they feel good again they must not have really loved their baby. Feeling better should not be a time for guilt. Parents are doing the hardest work of their lives - grieving.

Some families have said they know what they need to help heal their grief. It may be planting a tree in memory of their child or going over the events of the loss with the doctor or hospital staff who were with them when their infant was delivered. Others may name the baby, write a letter to the infant, or hold a memorial service. Parents should do whatever they feel will help them.

While there may be a strong drive within them to do these special things for their baby, there is nothing magical about planting a tree or visiting with the doctor. These events are bits and pieces that help parents in their healing, but they do not heal. As important as they are, these special activities will not take the grief away. There is no cookbook for healing.

When parents do begin to reorganize their lives, they notice a sense of calm and peace, renewed energy and interest, and the ability to make decisions. They are able to eat and sleep again. The loss will never be forgotten, but it becomes less painful.

This is the time when the "new normal" that parents feel may include a sense of their inner strength for having survived the terrible ordeal of grief.

AM I GRIEVING NORMALLY?

Parents often ask three questions when going through grief:
"Am I normal?"
"Am I going crazy?"
"Will I ever get over this?"
A better question is whether their grief is healthy. There is, of course, no one right way to grieve. Many of the strangest emotions and thoughts actually are quite normal. But even parents who grieve in a healthy manner have times when they are overwhelmed by their grief.

The following checklist may help parents figure out how they are doing. As time goes on parents will find they are answering yes to more and more questions. But if they are not satisfied with how they are doing, they should seek help.

☐ Am I able to laugh without feeling guilty?

☐ Do I pay attention to my personal appearance? (hair, clothes, make-up)

☐ Do I enjoy being out with friends for an evening?

☐ Am I feeling pleasure in sexual experiences?

☐ Am I able to sit quietly by myself and think of things other than the loss?

☐ Do I take an interest in current events and the news? (television or radio news, newspaper)

☐ Do I feel I can effectively parent my surviving children?

☐ Am I able to do the daily tasks I'm used to performing? (yard work, housework, cooking, household maintenance)

☐ Do I look forward to outings, trips, special events?

☐ Am I involved in activities that I participated in before the loss? (church work, volunteer work, clubs, sports teams, a job)

☐ Can I talk about the loss without showing strong emotion? (sadness, anger, jealousy)

☐ Do I feel like the fog has lifted?

☐ Do I pay attention to my surroundings? (beautiful scenery, the taste of food, the smell of perfume)

☐ Am I able to get a good night's sleep and awaken feeling rested?

☐ Am I able to concentrate on work and conversation?

☐ Am I less forgetful and better able to think clearly?

☐ Can I recall past events?

☐ Do I feel stronger and more in control? (less like an open wound, better able to cope with others' comments, better able to cope with everyday crises)

☐ Am I able to deal with everyday life without feeling panicked, frantic, or excessively worried? (minor injury to a child, someone arriving late, travel)

☐ Do I feel that there is meaning to my life?

☐ Can I look back at what happened and feel that something good came out of the tragedy?

SUGGESTIONS FOR DEALING WITH GRIEF

When a loss occurs, parents often search for ways to help themselves during grieving. Because of their inability to make decisions, they ask others for suggestions.

The following list came, in part, from research on mourning done by Glen Davidson, Ph.D. We have modified it to include ideas from our own experience in working with parents.

These are NOT answers, but suggestions. Parents can choose among these ideas and adapt them to their needs.

COMMUNICATION

• Talk about the baby and your feelings with your partner, family, and friends. It may sound trite, but this is an excellent outlet for releasing bottled-up emotions.

• Try to resume old and start new relationships as a couple and as individuals.

NUTRITION

• Eat a balanced diet that includes milk, meat, vegetables, fruit and whole grains.

• Avoid "junk" and fast foods.

FLUID INTAKE

• Drink 8 glasses of liquids (juice, water, soda) per day. It can be useful to keep a measured jug of water in the refrigerator to assure that you drink enough.

• Don't drink caffeine or alcohol because they may cause dehydration, headaches, and/or low back pain.

EXERCISE

• Do something active every day, such as biking, walking, jogging, aerobics, or stretching. Even a walk around the block can be useful.

TOBACCO AND ALCOHOL

• Avoid tobacco because it depletes the body of vitamins, increases acidity of the stomach, decreases circulation, and can cause palpitations.
• Don't drink alcoholic beverages because they depress body function and natural emotional expression.

REST

• Avoid increased work activity.
• Maintain rest patterns even if unable to sleep.

READING

• Read books, articles, and poems that provide understanding and comfort so you do not feel so alone.
• Avoid "scare" literature and technical medical publications.

WRITING

• Keep a diary or journal of thoughts, memories, and mementos.
• Write letters, notes, and/or poems to or about the baby.

PHYSICAL EXAM

• Schedule a physical examination about four months after experiencing a loss because the body is at risk of developing diseases during grief.

Big Decisions/Changes

- Don't move or change jobs or relationships. Wait 24 months before making these changes.
- Avoid long trips. Coping mechanisms and reflexes are impaired, making judgments difficult.
- Don't put away baby clothes until you are ready.
- Don't let others make decisions for you.

Help From Others

- Admit to yourself and family when you need help. This can lessen your pain and loneliness.
- Accept help from others. Let others know specific things they can do for you, such as providing food, company, or child care.
- Allow family and friends to share your grief and let them offer their support.
- Attend a support group. Couples who have "been there" can give support, help, and hope.

Faith

- Request help or support from your clergy to help renew your faith and hope.

"There's not one day that
rolls around that I don't remember."

LOVING AND REMEMBERING 22 YEARS LATER

*I*t was New Year's Eve and Frank was driving through a terrible snowstorm to take his stillborn daughter to a funeral home.

When his car stalled, Frank put his daughter under his coat and went to a nearby farm house to telephone for help. "I couldn't leave her in the car," he said later. "It was too cold."

The memory of those words are still with his wife, Judy, two decades later. Also vivid are the images of her three losses - from newborn death, stillbirth, and miscarriage. To this day, Judy still loves and wonders about her children who have died, just as she loves her three living children, Michael, Charles, and Elizabeth.

On Valentine's Day she thinks of her daughter, Donna Lynne, who died four days after her birth.

"It happened in February, just before Valentine's Day. That is why that holiday reminds me of her," she said.

But there also are many other days when Judy is reminded of Donna. "At church when there is a baby being baptized or a children's service, I picture what might have been. When Christmas rolls around . . . . There's not one day that rolls around that I don't remember."

Judy cries when she talks about her losses, but still she insists talking does not hurt her. They are her children even if they have died. She wants others to know about them and she wants parents who have lost children to know how important it is to talk.

Donna Lynne was full term, but doctors had no hope she would live because of an opening in her abdomen. "I didn't get to see her. The doctor wouldn't let me see her. He whisked her away to Iowa City." She was told her baby was "deformed," causing Judy to imagine a twisted head or body. But, when Judy saw Donna Lynne at the funeral, "she was beautiful. She had lots of hair."

Judy remembers, too, the events leading to her second loss. One night when she went to bed she no longer felt the movement from her baby who had become her nocturnal athlete. "Generally when I would go to bed, she would jump for joy. No matter how I lay that night, there was no movement." The next morning she still did not feel movement.

After the delivery, Judy remembers her doctor telling a nurse to "just throw it over in the corner." Judy, sad, exhausted and angry, responded, "Doctor, that is my baby you are talking about. He said he didn't mean that. But he did mean that. I wouldn't have him deliver another child of mine."

Judy never did see her second daughter. "I always wondered if she looked like the other one or if she resembled the boy. I was told she had lots of hair like the first one," she said. "I always wondered did they clean her up or just wrap her up and forget about her?"

Her third loss, a miscarriage, occurred about four months into the pregnancy. Again, she wonders and remembers.

When her last child, Elizabeth, was full term, Judy's labor was induced by a compassionate doctor who did not want Judy to worry any longer than necessary. "I felt good," Judy said, "that God finally let me keep a daughter."

BITTERSWEET GRIEF

O nce parents have worked their way through their grief they may find themselves experiencing these phases of grief again - but in shorter forms - on special dates, anniversary dates, holidays, during changes in seasons, at the birth of another baby, while talking to someone who has had a loss or to a parent of a child the same age as the baby who died.

This grief was termed "bittersweet" by Karren Kowalski, R.N., Ph.D., because memories of the child who has died cause both a sadness and a happiness. It occurs to parents throughout their lives. A small piece of the sorrow remains forever in the hearts of parents who have lost a child even after their lives have returned to their "new normal."

While most well-meaning people fear that mentioning the baby will cause the parents more pain, this is not the case. Parents want to think of and talk about their baby. Families and friends can help by remembering the baby in conversation and on special dates. They need to include the baby who has died as part of the family.

CHAPTER 2

*"It's very hard for me to think
that I am ending my childbearing
years with a death."*

GRIEF WITHIN A RELATIONSHIP

OUR GRIEF SEEMS SO DIFFERENT

It took a long time for Janet to realize Frank was grieving but just showing it differently. She grieved openly for a long, long time, while he appeared to be going on with his life.

"He changed all the door knobs in the house. We have new door knobs on every door in the house. He changed the outlets. We have new outlets and new switches in the house," Janet said. "He painted all the ceilings."

"How many of you have all new doorknobs?" she asked one night at a Resolve Through Sharing meeting. While no one had new doorknobs, the group laughed in understanding.

"At times," she continued, "I didn't think he felt the loss as much as I did, but I've learned that everybody, whether you are a mother or father, carries grief on an individual basis. This grief can't be compared to anyone else's grief. All of your feelings are unique and valid."

Janet and Frank also viewed the solution to their problems far differently.

"My first loss was an easy one to get through. I felt the empty arms and all of the things I feel now, but I knew there would be a faster end in sight," she said. "I knew another baby would be planned.

"My husband has decided to not have any more children. He says two is enough. It's very hard for me to think that I am ending my childbearing years with a death."

Janet believed the answer for her was a baby, which "really lightens some of the grief load."

Frank disagreed quietly, but adamantly, "What would happen if we went through that and the same thing happened that happened twice already?"

Frank and Janet's first and second losses were through miscarriage. They have two children, Frankie, eight, and Jacqueline, three-and-a-half. (They have since suffered another loss - an ectopic pregnancy.)

The differences between Frank and Janet go back to the second loss. While Janet wants and needs to talk about it, Frank does not. He always was "pretty quiet" about the loss. Frank said he felt the loss of his son at the time but doesn't "reflect on him a lot." While she remembers trying to "will him alive," he said he accepted his son was dead.

The couple has pictures of their son and his ultrasound, but Janet regrets she did not get to hold him. "I was in a state of shock, really relying on Frank to tell me what to do. I didn't know what to do or think. I listened to what the staff told us and they really didn't tell us too much.

"He had hair, dark hair, just the tiniest little tongue, the tiniest little penis. His legs were very skinny, not much muscle on them. Tiny, tiny ears. I was surprised he was so skinny. I could see his rib cage.

"It is only our tremendous love for each other that has helped us through the long months since the baby died. If we can make it through these last 21 months, we can make it through anything. At times I wonder how Frank can put up with my swings in moods."

INCONGRUENT GRIEF

It is a sad irony of grief that while two parents are suffering the loss of the baby, each expresses it differently. No two people - even those married or together a long time - react to a situation in the same way.

The differences can be explained, in part, by the differing roles society expects of men and women. Although our culture is changing, it still dictates that men should keep their emotions to themselves. This may make men appear unfeeling when, in reality, they are not.

"This is the point I couldn't get her to understand," a father said. "Fellows aren't supposed to cry, so I didn't cry. I grew up with that. Don't ask me to cry. Don't expect me to cry."

Attachments to the baby also may be different. A pregnant woman may think of the baby as part of herself, while the expectant father tends to think of the baby as a new individual. Since the baby is carried by the mother, she tends to feel closer to the baby sooner. Her thoughts often are on the baby and her pregnancy from the moment she learns she is expecting. A father may not have those feelings until closer to the time the baby is due or until after the baby is born.

"When I found out I was pregnant, I was excited. I began visualizing what the baby would look like," said a mother.

But her husband said he did not have many images of the baby. "Personally, I thought I would worry about it when the time came . . . . The first time I really realized I was going to be a father was in admissions when they asked me if we wanted our baby's birth announced in the newspaper. I asked 'Am I going to be a father tonight?'"

The expectant father tends to experience the pregnancy through what his partner tells him and by what he can see and feel. He has fewer experiences when the baby is lost early in a pregnancy because he has not felt or seen the body changes in his partner. "To me it was a collection of cells," one father said, "but to her it was a little girl."

Grieving is a very personal experience based on individual values and past experiences. It cannot be measured or compared; nor is one way of grieving better than another. Differences in how men and women grieve may be especially hard to understand for parents who are experiencing their first loss.

Some say women grieve the first year, while men, trying to hold their family together, shelve their feelings until the second year. As the anniversary of the death passes, fathers often realize what they are missing and how they have suppressed their feelings that first year. Their emotions often come out forcefully; sadness, anger and guilt are common.

Once parents recognize they are both grieving, but are just expressing it differently, they may be able to bridge the gap. Sharing feelings and thoughts comes easier to some couples than others. Some people are able to have honest, heart-to-heart talks. Others may need to write a letter to each other or express their feelings through a third person.

One mother wrote her husband a letter to open communication. She told him it upset her that he didn't cry. She thought he went to work so he wouldn't have to think about their baby. After reading the letter, her husband told her, "I don't stop thinking about it when I go to work. It bothers me. I may not cry a lot about it, but I think about it. It's just my way of dealing with it."

Couples need to share honest feelings with each other. Silence between them can build walls in the relationship.

Warning signs of trouble in a relationship are:

- spending more time at work
- an increase in drinking
- an affair
- over-involvement in church or other groups
- spending a large amount of time with parents, siblings, or friends
- doting on a surviving child
- prolonged lack of sexual activity
- hearing themselves say, "Yes, we talk all the time, but we NEVER GET ANYTHING RESOLVED."

Parents may wonder if they will ever grieve in the same way at the same time. The answer probably is no. In fact, they often take turns grieving. One takes care of business while the other grieves. Then, as the one begins to heal and can take on more responsibilities, the other one begins to grieve. Parents will always be two different people. But if they understand and accept each other's feelings, they can help one another heal.

THE EFFECT OF A
LOSS ON SEXUAL INTIMACY

W hen a couple loses a baby, they are affected in so many ways. The same intimacy that created their child may be difficult now. Or, they may find it a source of great strength. Whatever a couple's relationship was before the baby died, it more than likely will be different afterwards.

Sex may be a positive way of communicating, to express love, support, comfort, and tenderness for each other. Sexual response may be a way of compensating for the loss or the desire to have a baby.

"It was not a problem for us," one mother said. "We were far away from each other's feelings. We really needed that physical closeness. Sometimes, it felt that was the only thing we could count on. It was a few minutes when we could shut ourselves off and stop thinking about how bad we felt."

Another mother would not allow herself the pleasure of sex after losing a child, believing she should give up sexual enjoyment as a form of self-punishment or self-denial. "How can we possibly do this," she asked, "when our son lies buried just a few miles away?"

Sex may help some couples share grief and find comfort in each other, but it is not an answer or replacement for pain. Increased sexual activity, without working through grief, may only repress or delay the pain.

Some couples may feel sex means having a baby and, therefore, fear losing another child. "What used to be so much fun is now associated with pain," a mother said. "Do I want to do this if it will end up six months from now, nine months from now, hurting?" While some couples can communicate this feeling, others may be unable to talk about it, leaving their partner to interpret it as a "cold shoulder."

Some parents lose interest in sex because of a loss of self-confidence or feeling of inadequacy for having lost the child. This is particularly common when the loss occurs in a second marriage and when previous, healthy children have been born.

Some couples become obsessed with having another baby, perhaps tying their sexual activity to a temperature chart. The pitfall in this overwhelming desire to become pregnant is that, under all this pressure, couples can lose their drive for sex.

One of the signs of depression following a loss is a decreased sex drive. A spouse who constantly says "I'm too tired" or "I don't feel like it" may turn off future efforts to make love.

Some fathers feel a response described in the book, *Motherhood And Mourning*, by Larry G. Peppers and Ronald J. Knapp: "The first time we had sex after the baby died, I can remember I felt funny, very funny. It was like I was entering a place where a dead body had been."

Prior to resuming sexual relations, the couple should express their concerns about resuming sex, feelings about themselves and each other since the baby died, and fears about getting pregnant again. They need to decide together if they are ready and what to do if one of them decides halfway through that they are not.

Couples should understand:

• Most parents who have had a loss go through an intense period when they are obsessed with having another child. They need to wait until this emotion passes somewhat before becoming pregnant. One baby cannot replace another.

• Intimacy and sexual expression do not always have to end in intercourse. Satisfaction is possible through holding, caressing, and expressing tenderness. This form of sexual expression is crucial for couples to help each other heal.

• Sex does not have to mean having a baby. If birth control is acceptable, couples should use it.

• One loss does not mean another will occur. They should determine whether their fears of conceiving again are rational or irrational. Fears can be overcome by getting more information about the loss or by going through genetic counseling.

• Decisions should not be made by one partner, but by both together.

• Punishing themselves or each other is hurtful, not helpful. They must think about how realistic their guilt is and work through this normal stage of grief.

• A decreased sex drive can be a normal part of grief. Desires should return.

• Sex need not be routine even for couples who have sexual intercourse only when most likely to conceive. Spice and excitement and a change of scene may help.

THINKING ABOUT
ANOTHER PREGNANCY

Parents generally think about another pregnancy with mixed feelings. They wonder if they should open their heart to another child or protect themselves from the possibility of another loss. Some shift between wanting a child right now, this minute, and saying they just don't want one . . . ever. Some have a deep desire to share love, while others may be trying to replace the love they lost. These mixed emotions and desires are very normal.

Some parents believe their emptiness can only be filled with a child. "I grieve for wanting to feel life moving inside of me," a mother said. "I also fear not ever being able to have children, although there is nothing physical to suggest this."

The desire to quickly become pregnant again may arise from an urgent and intense need within the parents or from pressure from well-meaning friends. As one father shared, some fathers find themselves in a hurry to have another child. They want to see their partner get out of depression and believe this is an easy answer. Parents hear advice from just about everyone, telling them to wait, don't wait, don't have a child at all. Some hear such well-intentioned but hurtful comments as, "You're lucky you can get pregnant. You'll just have to try again." or, "You're still young. You can always have another baby."

Having another does not shorten grief. Replacing one loss with another child is impossible since each life is unique. Parents choosing to become pregnant again must welcome a new life with all the love the baby deserves as a new, separate individual. This may be difficult or even impossible until grief is resolved. "If we had had a baby right after Jessica died, it wouldn't have been a good thing," one mother said. "We would have been putting too much of what we wanted for Jessica on that baby."

Some parents become preoccupied with the thought of having another baby - right away. Having been told "You will know when it is right" to have a child, they believe these feelings indicate the time is right.

The preoccupation with having another baby, which some parents have described as an obsession, generally passes. But even many months later, they may feel having a child will rid them of the grief that may still linger.

For some parents, planning another child is a way to look to the future. Having a baby too soon, however, may make it difficult to feel close to the new baby.

Parents may wonder how they will know when they are ready. This is not an easy question to answer, since it varies so much from couple to couple.

It may be helpful for parents to ask themselves these questions.

- Does the loss still consume my every thought?

- Am I obsessed with becoming pregnant?

- Can I think about the loss without it tearing me apart?

- Am I able to once again find importance in other people and activities?

- Do I have happiness in my life, so that I can laugh and enjoy my life?

- Am I expecting this next child to make me feel better?

No one can decide for the couple, but if they give themselves time to heal and to think things through clearly they will be better able to make the decision. Physical conditions, such as age, health, and type of loss, should be considered. A woman's body must be ready to carry another pregnancy. The length of time for recovery will be different depending upon whether the loss was through miscarriage, ectopic pregnancy, stillbirth, or newborn death. It also will be longer if the mother had a Cesarean birth rather than a vaginal delivery.

Some couples, who were infertile or waited a long time to become pregnant, may feel an urgency to try again, particularly if they are in their 30s and feel the pressure of time.

The father and mother may disagree about when to begin a new pregnancy. The father may be willing to start as soon as possible after a miscarriage or ectopic pregnancy, while the mother is willing to wait. The couple is likely to agree about waiting if the loss was from stillbirth or newborn death. The number of losses also may affect how long the couple wants to wait.

Even after another baby is conceived, feelings may be mixed. "When I found out I was pregnant, I had mixed emotions," a mother said. "I was overjoyed, yet scared. I was happy as ever to think we were going to finally have another baby, but, at the same time, everything about our first baby's death kept haunting me."

Some mothers describe their feelings as a cloud hanging over the new pregnancy, especially until they pass the point at which death occurred in their previous pregnancy(ies). Instead of a happy, carefree feeling, the pregnancy may be clouded with constant reminders of the baby who died.

Couples need to share these normal feelings and concerns with others. Some couples find professional assistance useful, while others find help in talking with other parents who have had a loss and later given birth to another baby.

Parents will never forget the child who died, even in anticipating or experiencing a new pregnancy. The pain may return as they compare the infants, pregnancies, and the births.

Responses To The Loss Of A Baby

One of the best steps a mother and father can take after a loss is to talk to each other about their feelings. It is an easy thing to advise but often difficult to do. Couples may not know how to begin to talk about the many emotions they feel.

The following is a list of comments men and women have made to us about their feelings. Many parents have found it a helpful tool in opening communication with each other.

First, they individually marked the responses that applied to them. Then, they shared their responses with each other and talked about their differences and similarities.

This list also can be reassuring to parents who find themselves worrying about whether their thoughts are normal. Most likely, they will find their own thoughts on this list. As strange as they may seem, these ideas are common to many, many parents who have lost a baby.

Women's Checklist

☐ "I wonder if my partner feels badly about our baby. His grief doesn't seem as great as mine."

☐ "I'm pregnant again, but I'm afraid to tell anyone. I can't stand the pain of having to tell them something happened."

☐ "I feel so empty, emptier than I've ever felt before."

☐ "I don't like the body changes I've experienced since I was pregnant - I feel too fat/too thin; or my body is _____."

☐ "I have experienced unpleasant physical symptoms such as aching arms, fast heartbeat, fatigue, butterflies in my stomach, always nervous, or _____."

☐ "Nobody understands me anymore. I feel all alone sometimes."

☐ "I sometimes feel like I'll never feel normal again like I used to. Will I ever be the same?"

☐ "My mood can change so fast - one minute I'm up and the next I'm down. I feel like I can't keep up with it."

☐ "I find myself wishing to be protected and taken care of more than before."

☐ "I find myself feeling obsessed with getting pregnant again. It seems like I'd feel so much better if I could look forward to another baby."

☐ "I'm so afraid of getting pregnant again - I don't think I could go through this again."

☐ "I think about the baby all the time - it's like I can't get it out of my mind. I wonder if that's normal."

☐ "I hate having sex. How can we be doing that when our baby has died?"

☐ "Since the loss, my partner and I have sex more often. I wonder if that is normal."

☐ "I don't feel attractive anymore. I'm worried that my partner will lose interest in me."

☐ "I find myself having scary fantasies about my partner or surviving children being killed in an accident or something."

☐ "My dreams frighten me - they're so real. I dream about _____."

☐ "My breasts ache to nurse my baby. Sometimes I feel letdown of milk."

☐ "I keep thinking over and over 'what did I do to cause this? I must have done something.'"

☐ "We didn't really want to be pregnant. I'm wondering if that's why our baby died."

☐ "My partner and I seem to talk and talk but never get anything resolved."

☐ "I'm so afraid that I'll forget the baby."

☐ "I find that I can't concentrate - I'm forgetful and just can't seem to keep it all together. Am I going crazy?"

☐ "My partner and I don't talk about important issues. We don't seem to have as much in common anymore. We seem distant."

☐ "I know my partner has lots of feelings - why can't he talk to me about them?"

☐ "I'm jealous of pregnant women and women with babies. I see them everywhere."

☐ "Our friends (sister, brother, etc.) had a healthy baby at the same time our baby was due. How can I stand watching that child grow up?"

☐ "We can never seem to agree about what to do socially - one of us wants to go out and the other wants to stay home."

☐ "I've been sick a lot since the baby died. Does that have anything to do with grief?"

☐ "I find I want to talk and talk about the loss - more than anything else I need someone to listen to me."

☐ "I think a lot about what it would be like if I were still pregnant - I'd like to have a day when I could pretend I was pregnant."

☐ "I still look at maternity clothes and plan the baby's room - is that OK?"

☐ "We're both back at work, but I still seem to be doing most of the work at home. It isn't fair."

☐ "Sometimes I get so angry at the baby for doing this to me."

MEN'S CHECKLIST

☐ "I feel like so much weight is on my shoulders - everyone looks to me to be strong."

☐ "I'm afraid I'll make my partner feel worse if I show my emotions. So I keep them to myself."

☐ "I don't feel as badly about this as my partner does."

☐ "All she does is cry. I'm tired of seeing her sad."

☐ "I feel myself being turned off by my partner."

☐ "My partner and I don't have sex as often as we did before the baby died. I'd like to have sex more often but she doesn't want to."

☐ "I wonder if I did anything to cause the baby to die. Did I drink too much, have negative thoughts or _____?"

☐ "I find myself wishing we could be normal again - will that ever be?"

☐ "It's not always logical but I sometimes resent my partner since we lost the baby. She gets all the attention."

☐ "My partner seems to have withdrawn love from me and dwells on the fact that our baby died."

☐ "My partner seems to need much more than I can give right now in terms of attention and affection."

☐ "My partner and I seem more distant since we lost the baby. We don't talk about important issues, we don't seem to have as much in common anymore."

☐ "I'm concerned whether or not we should become pregnant again . . . . What will happen to us if we lose another baby?"

☐ "I think my partner would be happy again if we had a baby right away."

☐ "My attention needs are greater than they used to be. I feel like I have to compete with _____ for attention."

☐ "I didn't think we were ready to have a baby. I worry that my thoughts caused the death."

☐ "We can't agree on when to get pregnant again - it's starting to cause a conflict."

☐ "I'm experiencing unpleasant physical symptoms, such as inability to sleep, increased or decreased appetite, fast heartbeat, butterflies in my stomach, always nervous or _____."

☐ "I'm not able to concentrate on anything. I'm very forgetful. Is that normal?"

☐ "My dreams frighten me - they're so real. I dream about _____."

☐ "My partner and I seem to talk and talk, but never get anything resolved."

☐ "My partner seems to talk to _____ more than she does to me - why can't she share her feelings with me?"

☐ "I hate coming home from work and finding her depressed again. Can't we be happy once in a while?"

☐ "Our friends (sister, brother, etc.) had a healthy baby at the same time our baby was due. How can I stand watching that child grow up?"

☐ "I've been sick a lot since the baby died. Does that have anything to do with grief?"

☐ "I find that I want to talk and talk about the loss - more than anything else, I need someone to *listen* to me."

☐ "I am worried about how we are going to be financially - there are so many bills to pay."

☐ "I feel like such a failure. Other men have healthy babies - why couldn't I?"

CHAPTER 3

*"Then not having the baby is
the loneliest feeling I have ever had.
I have never been so lonely,
sad, empty, devastated."*

MISCARRIAGE

"It's like someone hit you in the gut 60 times."

After her miscarriage, Lee Ann wondered if she would make it through the next minute, let alone the next day. Day to day things like washing dishes and making beds went undone as she was wrapped up in her inner pain. "I remember sitting on the floor and crying and my husband coming home and finding me there."

Her husband, Daniel, also had difficulty functioning. "It's like someone hit you in the gut 60 times. It was devastating. I was really mad at God for a long time, but I got over it. I was really touchy with Lee Ann and not functioning well at work."

Lee Ann was surprised by the intensity of her feelings. Before her loss, she had minimized the impact of miscarriage. She never thought it could be traumatic because she, like many others, assumed the parents "never knew the baby." But Lee Ann and Daniel discovered they did know their baby who died about three months into the pregnancy.

"I never thought about the potential that child had until that child was not there. I remember thinking about what my child's little toes and fingers would look like. I wondered whether the baby would have my husband's big, brown, puppy-dog eyes or my squinty blue eyes."

Daniel, too, began thinking about the baby early on. Lee Ann said, "he would talk to my belly at night, tell the baby he loved him."

After Seth died, Lee Ann said they were lucky to have friends who would cry with them. Many friends encouraged them to talk. "That was the most important thing . . . I feel very, very sorry for the woman who holds it in and doesn't talk about it."

Some individuals said things that were hurtful, such as "You're young. You can have more kids." Lee Ann eventually recognized the comment, while thoughtless, was the individual's attempt to comfort her. But that kind of statement hurt because she felt, "This was my child. This was the one I wanted, not the more I can have in the future."

While Lee Ann and Daniel had friends who supported them, returning to work was difficult for both of them. Daniel was criticized for missing work following the miscarriage and no one allowed him to talk about his loss. Lee Ann said she was expected to return to normal life quickly. "I lost a child and they didn't understand why I was not back to normal after a week. I don't know how you can say, 'Oh, well,' and go on with life and not have it affect you."

Seth was so small — about an inch long — that Lee Ann and Daniel could not hold him. But they are comforted by the remembrances they have of their baby. They have pictues of Lee Ann during the pregnancy, cards from friends, and a basket of dried rose petals from the flowers friends sent to her in the hospital. Lee Ann wears a ring with a July birthstone. Engraved inside are Seth's name and birthdate.

These comforts are important for Lee Ann, but still do not take the place of the child she loved. "When I was pregnant, there was a very special feeling knowing I had life growing inside of me," she said. "Then not having the baby is the loneliest feeling I have ever had. I have never been so lonely, sad, empty, devastated."

Sometimes Devastating, Sometimes Not . . . Sometimes In Between

Miscarriage is like most things in life. There are as many ways to react to it as there are people.

Parents may mourn deeply, not at all, or somewhere in between. One mother may be devastated, calling it "the most terrible thing a family has to go through." Those who mourn little initially may mourn the baby months or years later. Other women may consider it just another learning experience. Some are relieved because they did not want to be pregnant. It is as normal for parents not to grieve as it is to be devastated by the miscarriage.

Research conducted by the authors found that 75 percent of women whose pregnancy ended in miscarriage grieved, while the other 25 percent considered it just another life experience. If a woman, in both her heart and mind, equated a pregnancy with a baby, she grieved for the child that was lost.

Parents who treat the miscarriage as a terrible event in their lives may be hurt by others who do not believe they should be so sad.

Miscarriages are more common than most people think. They occur in 15 to 20 percent of all pregnancies, usually between the seventh and 14th weeks.

In miscarriage, the couple is able to conceive, but something happens early in the pregnancy to cause the premature delivery. Miscarriage actually is a birth, and women feel pain much like that of childbirth. The delivery occurs because the uterus contracts and the cervix opens.

A miscarriage can occur quickly or over a long period of time. Women can spot or bleed, cramp a little or a lot. Mothers often are shocked by the amount of bleeding and pain they have during miscarriage. A dilatation and curettage (D&C), or scraping of the uterus, may be necessary when a miscarriage is incomplete or inevitable. The D&C is done to prevent prolonged bleeding and infection.

Following the pregnancy loss, the body takes weeks to return to normal. Breasts may be tender; milk may even come in. Uterine cramping may continue for several days. Bleeding or spotting may continue for a week or more. Heavy bleeding, a foul discharge, or a fever should be reported promptly to a physician or nurse-midwife.

Following a miscarriage, physicians often tell parents to just "wait and watch" in future pregnancies. Parents may interpret the doctor's comments as insensitive, but the physician may be trying to say that there is no way to treat or prevent most miscarriages.

While the impending miscarriage may be discovered early through ultrasound, this early diagnosis may mean parents will have the agony of waiting for the actual loss to occur. However, it also may give them the opportunity to avoid the physical trauma of a spontaneous miscarriage by having a D&C performed.

Many women search for a reason for their loss. Finding none, they turn to things they think they might have done. The following are known NOT to cause miscarriage:

- previous use of an IUD
- previous elective abortion
- use of oral contraceptives prior to conception
- work, exercise, or sports
- previous venereal disease or pelvic inflammatory disease
- sexual intercourse, in any position, during pregnancy
- occasional use of over-the-counter medicines or alcohol
- anxiety.

Most miscarriages are the result of unforeseen, unpreventable difficulties.

- Random, genetic errors. These result in incorrect development of the baby and are the major cause of miscarriage in the first 12 to 13 weeks of pregnancy. Most genetic errors do not repeat themselves. If they do, studies of the chromosomes of both the mother and father may be helpful.

- Low progesterone level. Without enough of this hormone, the lining of the uterus is not capable of caring for the fertilized egg. This low level can only be diagnosed before pregnancy has begun. A low hormone level can be treated in a subsequent pregnancy with natural progestin supplement soon after ovulation.

- Uterine structure. The structure of the uterus also can interfere with normal implantation of the egg. Problems could have been there since birth or caused by a growth or scar tissue from previous surgery. They can be diagnosed by X-ray or other tools to inspect the inside of the uterus.

• "Incompetent" cervix. This means the cervix opens prematurely and painlessly in the second or early third trimesters of pregnancy, causing premature birth of the baby. If detected, the problem may be prevented in future pregnancies by tightening the cervix with stitches.

• "Blighted ovum." This is an egg that develops abnormally because of a chromosome or genetic problem. Women who have a blighted ovum are pregnant, but the baby does not develop. The egg produces a placenta but not an embryo (the earliest stage in the development of a baby). This problem is unlikely to repeat itself or affect future pregnancies.

• Infections. Herpes, rubella or a bacteria-like pneumonia called mycoplasma, can cause miscarriages on rare occasions.

There are some other rare causes such as blood incompatibility or problems related to the immune system. Sometimes, no cause is found.

Most of the causes of miscarriage do not repeat themselves. Although careful medical attention may be necessary, a mother's chances of having a healthy baby after one or two miscarriages is about the same as if she had never had a miscarriage.

CHAPTER 4

"It was hard for me to start worrying about getting pregnant after all these years of worrying if I could get pregnant."

ECTOPIC PREGNANCY

AN EMOTIONAL MERRY-GO-ROUND

*T*here was a decided difference in the way Sue reacted to her first and second ectopic pregnancies.

With the first one, she did not even know she was pregnant until her Fallopian tube ruptured from the pressure of the fertilized egg growing inside. Then all she cared about was relief. "By the time I got to the operating room I was in so much pain, I could hardly wait until they knocked me out."

Because her tube ruptured, emergency surgery was required to remove it and an ovary, leaving her with an even more limited chance of conceiving than she had as an infertility patient. Sue had had a baby a few months earlier, but conceiving Skip only was possible because of microscopic surgery to open her blocked Fallopian tubes.

After her ectopic pregnancy, Sue viewed the loss as an experience she just had to get through. "It was like a biological accident. I was not trying to get pregnant. I was breastfeeding and not using birth control. It was hard for me to start worrying about getting pregnant after all these years of worrying if I could get pregnant."

Because of concern that she might become infertile again after the ectopic pregnancy, she and her husband, Jim, quickly tried to conceive once more. I had very strong feelings about having more than one child if I could," she explained. "I didn't want to raise an only child if it was at all possible."

Within months, Sue felt changes in her body that convinced her she was pregnant. A urine pregnancy test came back negative, however, and results from a blood test were "abnormal."

"I started spotting," Sue recalled. " I had a sense things were not going right. I was trying to tell myself it would be OK, but I knew in the back of my mind that something was not right."

Her doctor performed an ultrasound and discovered the fertilized egg had again implanted improperly. The baby was in her tube.

"I knew going in I was losing the baby. That was really hard. I remember waking up and crying about losing the baby," Sue said.

The sense of loss was much greater the second time because she had been anticipating the baby. "I was planning. I knew I was pregnant . . . . When I lost the baby, I lost a potential person. When a woman is pregnant, she fantasizes about what the baby is going to be like. I went through all that. Whether it would be a girl or a boy, whether it would have blond hair and blue eyes. I just didn't go through it for nine months."

After the second loss, Sue said she still did not express her emotions completely until a Resolve Through Sharing *counselor visited her. "I wasn't expressing my anger and depression like I could have. It all came pouring out one day."*

Sue has since had a second child, Amy. She and her husband will not try for another, knowing an ectopic pregnancy often can repeat itself and has in her life. "I don't know if I could put myself, my husband, and my family through this emotional merry-go-round."

FEARING FUTURE LOSSES
AS WELL

T he loss of any baby is difficult. But couples who have had an ectopic pregnancy may have an additional emotional burden. Just as the woman is recovering from major surgery, she and her partner may be mourning not only for their lost child but for future ones as well.

"With a tubal pregnancy," one woman explained, "there may be a greater feeling of loss because you worry about being able to conceive again."

Couples may not recognize the full impact of that loss initially. But after a time, some begin to feel sadness about the scar from surgery, the loss of a tube, or the loss of the pregnancy. Some begin to worry about ever conceiving again. Most of all, they may be confused by what exactly an ectopic pregnancy is.

In a normal pregnancy, the egg of the woman unites with the sperm of the man in the woman's Fallopian tube, travels down the tube, and implants in the uterus.

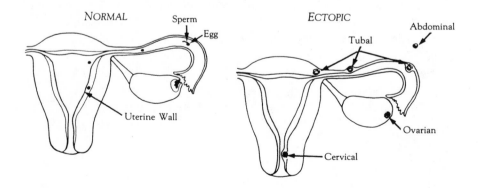

In an ectopic pregnancy, the fertilized egg implants somewhere else - usually in a Fallopian tube, but occasionally on the ovary, in the cervix, or abdomen.

Ectopic pregnancy differs from other losses because many couples are unaware they have conceived. An embryo pushing on a tiny Fallopian tube can cause great pain. Those who knew they were expecting a baby may have noticed common symptoms of pregnancy. Those who didn't know they were pregnant may be alarmed by the pain.

With the use of ultrasound and serum pregnancy testing, ectopic pregnancy has become easier to diagnose. A doctor begins looking for an ectopic pregnancy if the woman has pelvic pain, dizziness and fainting, decreased blood pressure, vaginal spotting or bleeding. Often women must have a number of tests and examinations while in severe pain. This time can be frustrating to couples who are desperate to find a reason for the pain. It is equally overwhelming to couples how quickly their doctor, once the diagnosis is confirmed, decides to operate. Immediate treatment is necessary because an ectopic pregnancy is potentially life threatening for the woman and nearly always requires surgery.

This may be the first time the woman has been hospitalized or had surgery. It also can be a frightening time for the people involved with her. They may feel helpless and intimidated by the hospital and very worried about her. Men worry about not having done something sooner, about not being able to see their partners before surgery, and fear their loved one may die.

Women are sometimes frustrated because their doctors and family treat the event as a surgical procedure, not as the loss of a baby.

A doctor may be able to find a cause for an ectopic pregnancy, although this is not always possible. Some causes are pelvic infections, endometriosis, congenital abnormalities of the Fallopian tube, previous tubal surgery, or adhesions.

Sometimes the Fallopian tube can be saved during surgery, but if it has to be removed during surgery, parents may mourn for this separate loss.

CHAPTER 5

*"It is a very weird feeling
to have a dead baby inside of you . . ."*

STILLBIRTH

*"You just pray and hope
they have made a mistake."*

---

*E*verything was going fine in Judy's pregnancy until a week
after her due date. Suddenly there was no heartbeat. An ultrasound
confirmed the baby's death.

The five-year dream of having a baby turned into a nightmare for
Judy and Rich. Particularly difficult was the wait for labor to begin
naturally. Induced labor and Cesarean section were considered too risky
for her health.

"It is a very weird feeling to have a dead baby inside of you," Judy
said. "You just pray and hope they have made a mistake. Even up
until the time you start labor and the baby is born, you wait for
the cry."

During those terrible four days until labor began, Judy didn't want to leave the house. "I was afraid people would ask me when my baby was due and I would have to tell them that the baby had died."

Judy remembers mixed feelings during labor. "When labor started, I didn't want to push. I just wanted to keep it inside. I hoped that if labor didn't start, I could keep it inside permanently."

It felt natural to want to hold Aimee after she was born, Judy said. "You automatically want to do it because you are that child's mother. You want her. Your arms want her if she is alive or isn't. That is the only time you will have with that child."

Judy said she will treasure both that hour-and-a-half she had with Aimee and the pictures taken of her by hospital staff. "I found myself, every night before I went to bed, pulling out her pictures that were taken at the hospital. I literally sat down and talked to her as if she was alive. Rich thought it was bizarre."

Holding Aimee and having pictures helped Rich as well. "I am glad we did do it now. I talked to other parents who wished they had a picture of their child," he said. "A lot of people didn't get to hold their baby."

The desire for a child is a very intense one for Judy.

"It's my life. I feel that my main purpose in life is to have a child that I will be able to hold and care for and live with me and share my life and happiness and sorrows with," she said. "I feel that is my role on this earth, and that is what I have always wanted."

The differences in the way the couple grieved later created problems for them. "I got so angry at him," Judy said, "I threw a book at him."

"I didn't show my feelings like Judy did when we first found out," Rich explained. "I found out I shouldn't have done that, but I did."

Judy is convinced parents need to know that it is normal to think and feel strange things following a loss. "I had a dream Aimee was lying in her coffin in my kitchen sink. The top was off. Her arms and legs were flying and moving around. It made me want to go the cemetery to see if she was really dead."

Judy also realizes it is normal to grieve for a baby for many months. "She was my child from the minute she was conceived. I carried that child for nine months. I felt that child kicking and moving around. I did know that child. I was her mother."

A Broken Promise Of Birth

In a stillbirth, the promise of nine months of pregnancy is broken when the baby is born dead. Perhaps the most difficult time for mothers is the time between learning their baby has died and delivering the infant. Psychologically, mothers feel trapped, frustrated and, sometimes, horrified that they are carrying a dead baby.

The rate of stillbirth has remained relatively unchanged in recent years. There still is no good explanation for why one in 110 babies is born dead.

Stillbirth cannot be anticipated in most cases, and even an autopsy may not always provide the answers. But, all efforts must be made to learn the cause. Parents need the information to rid themselves of guilt that often accompanies this loss. They need to be reassured that the problem will not repeat itself in future pregnancies. The baby's siblings need to know if the problem could be inherited.

Some causes for stillbirth are:

- genetic or chromosomal abnormalities of the baby
- complications from Preeclampsia (Toxemia)
- placental abruption or when the placenta separates from the baby
- complications of the umbilical cord
- diabetes in the mother (a less frequent cause today than in earlier times)
- other medical disorders of the mother.

The majority of women who have a stillbirth become pregnant again and give birth to live children. Even though the risk of a second stillbirth is very small, the shock of a stillbirth runs deep and continues through later pregnancies.

CHAPTER 6

"Every time we walked in and saw him, we prayed so hard God would take him; and every time we walked out, we would pray God would let him live."

NEWBORN DEATH

SOMETIMES LOVE REQUIRES SAYING GOOD-BYE

*D*eath was the last thing in Debbie's and Dave's thoughts when their son, Eric, was born. The labor and delivery had gone well. Family and friends had begun to visit and bring gifts. "But I had an uneasy feeling in the back of my mind. The doctors had a hard time getting him to stay pink. I didn't feel reassured by what the doctors were saying. I was afraid of brain damage," Debbie said. "The staff looked at me like I was off the wall."

The next morning a nurse woke her and said, "Eric's turning blue." Debbie called Dave, who was home with their two-year-old son, Chad. "I burst out crying and said," "Dave, there's something wrong with Eric." "He jumped up and literally flew to the hospital."

Tests showed a congenital heart condition. "They said right away it was serious, extremely serious, that it didn't look good."

After Eric was stabilized, he was moved to the hospital's neonatal intensive care unit. "Once we were in NICU, the real nightmare began," Dave said. "He was hooked up. An IV was going into his navel and a breathing tube was going down his mouth. A drainage tube was in his stomach so if he happened to get any air in his stomach they could pump it out." Eric also was on a heart monitor and oxygen.

The NICU staff just worked around child and parents. "That was most important. They realized we needed to be there and the contact between the parents and that child was so important," Dave said. "They wanted us to hold the baby, even if we couldn't. They said it was so important."

Debbie and Dave remember having mixed feelings in NICU. "Every time we walked in and saw him, we prayed so hard God would take him; and every time we walked out, we would pray God would let him live."

On the third day, the doctors said the couple had to decide if they wanted to continue to try everything possible to prolong Eric's life or to let him die naturally. "We had the choice of whether we wanted to buy time and keep him artificially alive and hope for a miracle overnight or just let him die on his own," Dave said. After a long talk, they decided Eric should die naturally, rather than have his life prolonged without hope that he would make it.

Doctors and nurses removed the equipment from Eric, wrapped him in a warm blanket, and brought him to a family room where the three of them could be together. Grandparents also came in and pictures were taken.

"About an hour after he was unhooked, when the medication wore off, he opened his eyes and looked at us. He stuck his finger in his mouth and started sucking," Debbie said. "He more or less went back to sleep." Towards the end, Debbie and Dave feared he was in pain, but a nurse said Eric was in a coma and felt nothing.

When he did die, Eric "looked like he was just sleeping." Debbie said, "I was scared because he was dead, but I didn't want to give him up. I just wanted to hold him."

A POIGNANT PAIN

When a newborn dies, there is a poignant pain. The promise of birth has been fulfilled and then is cruelly snatched away. The period between the living birth and the finality of death is often filled with anxious waiting.

Parents have a need to spend time with their youngster, but the special care the baby needs may make this difficult. Mothers and fathers need to "parent" their baby, regardless of the condition of the youngster. They need to feel that they are a family, regardless of the limited time they have. Parents should be allowed and encouraged to give as much care as possible during this time, such as changing the baby's diaper. Touch also is extremely important. Touching and holding the baby can develop that important bond between parent and child.

Sometimes parents must be involved in deciding whether or not a severely disabled or abnormal baby should be kept alive through extraordinary care. The trauma of giving birth, anxiously waiting to see if the baby will live, and the need for making life and death decisions are all part of the grief of parents whose longed-for baby dies soon after birth.

Causes of newborn death include:

• Problems associated with prematurity. The tiny baby's systems are just too immature to live. The lungs may not be able to give the baby the air he needs or the immune system may not be able to fight off infection.

• Abnormalities that are incompatible with life, such as severe defects of the heart, brain, kidneys, lungs or endocrine system.

CHAPTER 7

*"We are grieving and loving
at the same time . . .
but it's not like pulling and tugging.
It's more like ripping and tearing."*

LOSS IN A
MULTIPLE PREGNANCY

GRIEVING AND LOVING
AT THE SAME TIME

*W*hen Michael and Marie learned that one of their twins
would be stillborn, they grieved intensely for the loss in their lives.

Later, they began to realize that Mason's death would have an even
greater effect on his twin sister, Briana. She would have to go through
life without the brother she had known since conception. "There are
lots of times that Briana starts to cry really loud for no reason at all,"
Michael said. "I know all babies do that, but it is such a sorrowful
cry that sometimes I think it is because she misses Mason."

As she held six-month-old Briana, Marie worried about the impact of
her brother's loss on her. Does she feel her parents' torment? Will she
feel guilty or angry about her brother's death? Will she feel that she
has been short-changed by that loss? Or, will she simply feel that

someone or something is missing? "She knew him better than any of us. She lived with him for nine months. She surely must feel that loss."

The story of Michael's and Marie's loss is a particularly poignant one because Marie, a maternal nurse practitioner, works with high risk pregnant women. When she learned she was to have twins, she realized her own pregnancy suddenly was high risk.

But her spirits were buoyed by having those with whom she worked caring for her. Loving co-workers/friends gave her special support before and after they learned Mason died.

Having more knowledge about pregnancy was a "double-edged sword," Marie said. She knew what to do to take care of herself and the babies and what could go wrong. She also had knowledge and experience in caring for parents who had lost a baby.

When she recognized signs of premature labor, Marie went to bed as her doctor ordered because she knew from experience how important bedrest could be. At that time Mason was alive. Now she wonders if he would have survived if she had gone into labor early.

The loss is extremely difficult because it involves such an emotional seesaw. "We are grieving and loving at the same time," Marie said. "But it's not like pulling and tugging. It's more like ripping and tearing. There are two violently different pulls. One minute I am sitting and nursing my daughter and the next minute, I am crying uncontrollably because I lost the other part of her."

Each day they look lovingly at Briana, proudly watching her face light up with a smile. But in that smile, they see the son they lost. "When you have a baby who looked exactly like her brother at birth, you can't look at her and not wonder what her brother would have looked like."

Every time Briana reaches a new developmental level, it is a reminder that Mason will never make that step. It is almost too difficult to look ahead to Briana's first birthday as it also will be the first anniversary of her brother's death.

Add to this devastating mixture the lost joy of parenting twins and the combination can be unbearable.

"It is not like we lost just one baby. We lost one of twins and the parenting of twins, the whole mystique of twins," Marie said. "We lost something unique. We had always felt very special because we were blessed with being the parents of twins."

Nighttime feedings are particularly difficult as Marie nurses Briana and thinks about her expectation of juggling the nighttime needs of two infants. She holds a baby in her arms, yet she still has the "aching arms" that parents report after losing a baby. Her arms were prepared for two.

Marie felt suspended in time during the early months following the loss. "I feel like I am not parenting or grieving well, but that I am doing a half job on both," Marie said. "I look at this gorgeous little face and don't want her to suffer because a large part of my heart and soul is grieving the loss of her brother."

Even more tormenting is the reaction many people have to the loss. Their entire town seemed to share their joy and excitement about having twins, yet there was only silence after Mason died. "No one came over right away. People didn't know what to say so they stayed away," Michael said.

Some people still ignore Mason's death and concentrate on Briana's birth. Others almost lecture the couple that they "should" feel happy because "at least" they have a daughter.

It doesn't matter which comes first — an expression of congratulations for Briana or sympathy for Mason — but Michael and Marie feel strongly that both are necessary. "Don't deny he was ours," Michael said, with Marie adding, "You can't deny the fact that Mason was a part of us, a part of our love, a part of Briana."

Still, Michael and Marie realize "the only way Mason will be remembered is if we keep people remembering that we had him. He will not be relegated to a corner of our lives. He will not be like a toy tossed aside. He will always be a part of us."

When All The Babies Don't Survive

When one baby, or more, in a multiple pregnancy dies, a mixture of conflicting emotions is created. Love and grief; reminders of life and death occur simultaneously every day, almost every minute.

The carrying of more than one baby gives a pregnancy a special excitement. Once parents learn they will have a multiple birth, they receive more attention than they normally would in pregnancy. They even experience a certain amount of added prestige.

The sudden loss of prestige after a death is difficult to handle. It is common in hospital nurseries to place signs on the babies' cribs indicating "Twin A" and "Twin B." One couple was deeply hurt after their Twin A died because the sign for Twin B was quickly removed. The parents felt this action denied them the recognition of having had twins because it was no longer difficult to distinguish between the two.

Parents know their babies as individuals. With the availability of ultrasound, they increasingly have become able to distinguish between their babies even before birth. To suddenly lose the baby's identity as part of a multiple birth can be very painful.

Some parents describe the feeling as having part of a baby die and part of a baby survive. They may see their children as a single entity. Part of their grieving process involves separating their babies and coming to terms with them as individuals.

One mother told the story of strolling two babies in the park. A woman came up and commented about how cute her "twins" were. The mother yelled, "No, they're triplets and one died."

If one baby, or more, dies parents suddenly find themselves torn between emotions. How can they celebrate life and mourn death at the same time? How do they say hello and good-bye simultaneously?

Parents find themselves feeling happy one moment because they have a live baby yet sad the next because another died. The thrill of watching their baby grow is tarnished with the constant reminder that they had expected to observe the development of more than one child.

A loss of one baby, or more, increases the feeling of vulnerability couples have, especially about the survivors. After one or more dies, parents may suddenly worry that if a bad thing could happen to them once, it could again. Many develop intense fears about the survivors, wondering if they can leave them alone or if they should have a nighttime vigil in the nursery.

It is not unusual for parents who have experienced life and death in a multiple birth to have the fleeting thought that it would have been better if all had died. They might feel their lives would be in less turmoil if they didn't have to grieve and parent simultaneously; that they would do a better job if they had just one emotional job to do — grieve. Parents must be reassured that these are normal feelings.

Parents who suffer a loss must take time to grieve. There is no way to shorten this process, even with the other child(ren) to love. One child does not make up for the loss of another.

One of the special problems in a multiple pregnancy when one baby, or more, dies is the reaction of the survivor(s). It is impossible to know what is in the mind of so tiny a baby, but, having shared the womb for nine months with a brother or sister, the baby may sense that someone is missing.

It is not unusual for a survivor, even one who did not know about the loss, to have a sense "someone is missing." A young, surviving twin may draw two people in self-portraits, even if she didn't know that she was a twin. Sometimes, sketches have parts missing. Older survivors of multiple pregnancies describe feeling that a part of them is not there. A five-year-old boy who had not been told that he had had a twin brother suddenly asked his mother, "Was I born alone?" Two years later, while flying on an airplane, the boy looked out the window and asked, "Do you think Chris looks like me? What do you think he likes to play in heaven?"

A surviving child sometimes feels guilty for living. He or she may feel somehow responsible for the sibling's death. Another common question is "Why did I survive?"

Parents need to tell their child as young as possible that there was one child, or more, who died. They need to be open to questions and accepting of unusual feelings from the youngster. The survivor may need reassurance that he did nothing to cause his brother or sister to die. He needs to understand that his parents could not have prevented the death either.

Parents may find their family and friends dwelling on the survivor(s) and ignoring the one(s) who died. "You're lucky you have one" is a common though hurtful response from others. This generally is done with the best of intentions. Loved ones fear they will inflict more pain by causing the mother or father to think about the one(s) who died.

Parents have to set the example by talking about and remembering their infant(s). They should tell their family how much it helps them to talk because they are thinking about the baby who died, regardless of whether others mention him. It is important, too, for parents to explain that they feel grief and joy at the same time.

Parents have said meaningful gifts make reference to all the children. Two or more trees can be planted at the home - to remember those who died and to grow along with the other child(ren). An outfit with multiple hearts also can be a fitting reminder for a multiple birth. One father of twins, one of whom died, gave his wife a pair of birthstone earrings - each earring symbolizing a baby.

Birthdays can be a time of remembering, too. There is no one right way to observe this day. Families may mark the occasion with a cake for those who lived and a visit to the grave of those who did not. Others have cakes for each of the babies. One family, at the suggestion of the living children, makes an angel cake for the baby who died.

Other families celebrate the birthday of the survivor(s) and reserve the remembrance of the other infant(s) for other times.

As time passes, some families make up for the obvious absence in their family album of those who died by having an artist draw what the child(ren) might have looked like at any given age.

The baby who has died is never forgotten by the parents. This continuing love needs to be recognized by others just as it is for those children who are living.

CHAPTER 8

"On a day filled with sorrow,
tears hard to dry.
With you go our hopes,
our love and our dreams."

SAYING GOOD-BYE

"With you go our hopes, our love and our dreams."

After each of Janenne and Galen's sons died through miscarriage, they did as much as they could for Michael and Christopher, as a sign of their love. Instead of using a hearse, "we drove each of our boys home to be buried. We had four hours in the car with each of them," Galen said. "It gave us time to sit and be with them."

Galen's father helped him dig the grave for Christopher. "Dad said, 'I am going to do it. I want to do it for my grandson.' It felt so good to hear him say, 'my grandson.'"

The deaths were shocking to the couple. They each come from large families where only one pregnancy had ended in a stillbirth. "We never really expected anything to go wrong. We were really excited about the

*prospect of having children," Janenne said. "My whole thing was
sitting with the baby, rocking and reading stories and playing games."*

The first miscarriage was very fast. The sudden onset of bleeding
was followed by the even more sudden miscarriage of Michael.

In sharp contrast was the time Janenne had to wait and prepare for
the miscarriage of Christopher after an ultrasound confirmed his death.
"We both started crying. We didn't see the heartbeat (on the machine),
and we knew it should be there," Janenne said. "We did get a picture
of the baby, and the baby wasn't moving at all."

Janenne was discharged from the hospital to recuperate and wait for
the expected miscarriage. "We had a week to prepare ourselves for
what was going to happen," she said. During that week she wrote her
son a poem, Forever, Christopher. "I stayed home and worked on
that one line at a time. I would do one line and then have to do
something else. I couldn't do anything then but cry."

Forever, Christopher

*Our tiny little baby, to whom we say good-bye.
On a day filled with sorrow, tears hard to dry.
With you go our hopes, our love and our dreams,
Of all life's beautiful things, we wanted you to see.
You are truly our son, our second baby born,
But from our loving arms; you were too early torn.
We'll never know the joy of hearing your first cry,
Of hearing your happy laughter, seeing the first step you try.
Christopher we love you; in our hearts you will remain
Our arms feel so empty, our lives won't be the same,
We will see you someday in heaven and hold you in our arms.
'Till then you remain a sweet memory, a baby, forever ours.
Christopher Jon Lingl*

JANENNE LINGL

After her babies died, Janenne wondered whether she was grieving
properly. "I can remember thinking that I would never feel any better.
I was wondering what was wrong with me because I was still crying
about this when it was over and done with."

It is important for parents to be prepared for the feelings they will have following this kind of a loss, according to Janenne. "There are going to be hard and terrible days. You don't know how you will possibly make it until tomorrow."

"Or," added Galen, "why you would even want to make it until tomorrow."

The couple's friends tried to be encouraging after the first loss, telling them to try for another baby. Their comments hurt, according to Janenne. "They took away the fact that the baby meant something to us, just by saying we could have another."

The couple did have another baby about a year later. She is healthy and happy, but she does not take the place of Michael or Christopher.

"She didn't take away my grief," Galen said. "In one way she made the grief more of a reality for me. Now that we have a living child, I know what I missed with the two boys. On the other hand it is nice to finally, after all this, be able to have a living child."

SAYING HELLO
BEFORE SAYING GOOD-BYE

Saying good-bye to a baby who has died through miscarriage, ectopic pregnancy, stillbirth, or newborn death is exceedingly difficult. Not only must parents say good-bye to a part of them, but they also must say good-bye to a dream. All this occurs before they were able to say hello.

"I knew I had to say good-bye, but I hadn't said hello yet," a father said. "I had to say to him I loved him before I could even think about him going."

There is no one right way for parents to say their good-bye. They should be encouraged to make their own choices when showing their love for their baby.

GIVING A NAME

Naming the baby comforts many parents, even when the loss was so early in pregnancy that the sex could not be determined. The name can be one originally planned or one that could fit either a son or daughter. Parents also should feel free to not give a name or to save the name for a subsequent child.

One mother, whose child died in the 10th week of an ectopic pregnancy, gave the baby a girl's name because she had a strong feeling the baby was a girl. "It was something I had to do! I feel closer to her now, and knowing her name has made it easier in talking to others about her."

EXPRESSING FEELINGS

Some parents express their feelings in a letter, poem, or story written about and for their baby. It can show their hope and love for the baby as well as the disbelief, anger, disillusionment, and despair they feel. A small sense of peace may come through writing or recording one's feelings, regardless of whether the words are shared or kept private.

SAVING MEMENTOS

Others set aside an item chosen especially for this baby as a loving tribute to their hopes and dreams. It may be a favorite maternity top, a special blanket, or a stuffed animal.

Other keepsakes include the baby's identification bands, footprints, crib card, a lock of hair, or the blanket or clothing the baby was dressed in. If the clothing is sealed in a plastic bag, the smell of the baby will remain longer. These items often are put into a memory book or chest for the baby.

One mother had a ring with the baby's birthstone engraved with his name and the date she miscarried. Some parents honor their baby by planting trees and flowers, symbols of the love they had hoped to give.

Pictures taken at the hospital and funeral home can become prized possessions. Some hospitals keep photographs on file until the family wants them. Parents also can take pictures.

Parents have said these mementos help preserve the memory of their baby, provide a feeling of closeness to him, and make the loss seem more real.

SEEING AND HOLDING THE BABY

Many parents find comfort in seeing and holding their baby. If this opportunity is not offered, they should ask for it. They should take as much time and as many opportunities as they need to hold and touch the baby or just look at her. They also should ask for privacy if it isn't offered.

It is not unusual for parents to be afraid to see their baby. A nurse can describe how the baby may look and feel and answer any questions.

If a couple did not see their baby while in the hospital, they usually can do so in the funeral home. Though it may be difficult, doing so may help them face the loss and relieve uncertainties about how the baby really looked.

"I looked to the chaplain for some feedback," a mother remembered. "His response, which was a very good one and helped me make up my mind, was 'Of all the people I have ever worked with that have chosen to see their babies, I don't know of anyone who has regretted it.'"

Grandparents and other children also can see and hold the baby if the family wishes. The staff should help with the arrangements.

Some parents want to bathe and dress their infant in clothing especially for their baby as a way to express their love. They should ask to do this if they wish to do so.

Putting Away Baby Things

One of the difficult tasks parents face is putting away maternity clothes and baby things. It need not be done right away, but, when it is done, the parents should do it as a couple. Friends may try to "protect" them by doing it for them, but the task will help parents face their loss and express their feelings.

Making Final Arrangements

The pain and confusion parents feel may make it hard for them to think about the final arrangements for their baby. They should ask as many questions and explore as many options as they wish. Then parents should make their own decisions. The planning will help them face the loss and begin grieving.

Whatever they do in caring for their baby's remains should depend upon how they feel and what they need. It should not depend on their baby's age at death.

A number of choices are available, including burial and cremation. If the baby is younger than 20 weeks gestation, the hospital can, if the parents wish, take care of the remains, generally by cremation.

One family whose baby died before the 20th week of pregnancy held a memorial service in the mother's hospital room. Immediate family members were present, and a local minister performed the service. Their baby, swaddled in a warm blanket, was brought to the mother's room. "Just to know she was there with us during the service helped us to say good-bye," the mother said. "The service provided us with a feeling of closure from the past two days' experience, though we knew her loss would keep on hurting for many days to come."

Parents can write and conduct the service themselves or ask a minister or other comforting person to do so. A prayer or blessing also may be said in memory of the baby, especially when baptism is not possible or desirable.

A funeral, either public or private, is another option. It may be at the graveside, a church, the hospital, or at home. Usually, the cost of a baby's funeral is much less than an adult's.

Parents who plan to have the service in a community other than the one in which they live may find it helpful to consult a funeral director from the town in which burial will take place. Parents may transport their infant themselves to help reduce expenses and to give them an opportunity to care for their baby.

Families may want to include a gift of flowers or a stuffed animal for their baby. This gift can be a way of helping siblings participate in the funeral, express their love, and begin to work through their grief.

As parents make final arrangements, they may find some funeral directors supporting their choices, while others will not. The responses from funeral directors are as individual as they are. Parents need to tell funeral directors what gives them comfort.

There are no right or wrong choices. Parents should let their heart and feelings guide them. They also should not let well-meaning people, including funeral directors, persuade them to do things that are uncomfortable for them. If the parents give in, they may have regrets later.

As parents plan the final arrangements for their child, they should think of this as an opportunity to give a gift of love. As Doug Manning, a minister and counselor, says in his book, *Don't Take My Grief Away from Me*, "The perspective should be: I am now called upon to plan a fitting memorial to a life. I should plan this memorial as I think and feel it should be done. The planning and the memorial are my gifts to this life. It is my way of expressing how I feel and what the person meant to me."

Even when parents do what is right for them, the pain does not disappear. They still will grieve — even with the best hello and good-bye they can give.

CHAPTER 9

*"I don't really remember
anybody saying anything that
made me feel better."*

Reactions Of Others

What Do You Say?

It did not take long for Kathie and Fred to realize many of those around them were not going to react to the death of their baby the way they wanted. Within an hour of their daughter's stillbirth, a nurse rushed into the room where Kathie was recovering. "We have to use your phone," the nurse said, "some people have happy news to share."

Until labor began, Kathie and Fred thought they would be the ones with happy news. Then a nurse did not find a heartbeat. An ultrasound confirmed the baby had died.

Jessica "looked fine" when she was born. "You couldn't tell anything was wrong," Kathie said.

After Jessica was stillborn, Kathie asked to be moved off the obstetrics floor and for something to calm her down. "I remember hearing other babies crying and the excitement of the lady who delivered right after me and everyone smiling and happy. We felt like we were intruders and we wanted out of there."

Her doctor refused to give her a sedative. Eventually, Fred snuck in a thermos of wine to "take the edge off" Kathie's pain.

The staff did not help relieve the pain she was feeling following that terrible loss, Kathie said. "The nurses would come in and pat me on the shoulder and say 'you can always have another.' I have an infertility problem. Knowing how long it took to conceive Jessica, we didn't know if another baby was in our future."

Some staff members did not know Kathie had lost her baby. A nurse asked her how her baby was doing, and a volunteer offered to take her baby's picture.

She had several problems with her doctor. After the ultrasound showed Jessica had died, he just left the room. "I wanted him to stay with us and cry with us." When her doctor later saw her smoking, he made her feel guilty by saying, "Maybe next time you're pregnant, you won't smoke."

Some of Kathie's friends came to see her, while others ignored her. "I don't really remember anybody saying anything that made me feel better." Comments about how good Kathie looked also were difficult to accept. "That really bothered me. I didn't want to look good. I felt so terrible."

Kathie and Fred were most angry about remarks from a priest who told them their loss was a burden God wanted them to carry as a form of punishment; that he understood their pain because he once had had a broken leg; and "Do not despair. You have an angel in heaven." Kathie responded, "I don't want her there. I want her here."

The biggest difficulty in dealing with the reactions of others was the realization that others thought Kathie and Fred should be "over" Jessica's death.

"We will never forget her," Fred said. "The memory is there. The pain is still there and the love is still there." Added Kathie, "Everybody puts a time limit on how long your grief should last. A lot depends on how long the baby lived. They feel you don't have memories. That is why people give you a time limit. What they forget is you were planning the memories in your mind. You were planning the baptism, the first word. That is part of the pregnancy."

The best a friend can do, according to Kathie, is say, "'I'm sorry' and sit with you and not try to change the subject. Let you talk."

It was after a group meeting of Resolve Through Sharing that Kathie wrote this poem.

What Do You Say . . .

What do you say when a baby dies and someone says . . .
  "At least you didn't bring it home."
What do you say when a baby is stillborn and someone says . . .
  "At least it never lived."
What do you say when a mother of three says . . .
  "Think of all the time you'll have."
What do you say when so many say . . .
  "You can always have another . . ."
  "At least you never knew it . . ."
  "You have your whole life ahead of you . . ."
  "You have an angel in heaven . . ."
What do you say when someone says . . . nothing?
What do you say when someone says . . .
  "I'm sorry."
You say, with grateful tears and warm embrace,
  "Thank you!"

                                        KATHIE MAYO

Long after that poem was written, Kathie said she developed a greater understanding and compassion for the people who made comments that appeared so hurtful after Jessica died. "Now I know they were doing the best they could."

BEING THERE . . .
IT'S A TOUGH ROLE

The loss of a baby touches friends and relatives, but they respond in many different ways. Some share tears with the parents, while others listen to them talk. Some friends avoid the parents and do not acknowledge the baby's death. Others visit but only talk about trivial things. At times, people say things that seem downright insensitive and cruel.

The problem, quite simply, is that most people do not know how to express their sympathy. Many people - until it happens to them - believe the loss of an infant is less than that of an older child or an adult. They expect parents' grief to be short-lived and temporary and think parents should erase their memories and move on.

Some people fear saying or doing the wrong thing, while others are frightened or uncomfortable about seeing the parents cry. Still others do not want to impose on the parents, thinking they have enough support from family and friends. They express their support with cards or gifts because they are uncomfortable talking.

Some people feel the need to answer for the parents' grief. They feel they must give a reason for the loss. **Family members and friends may not realize they help by just listening - and not offering a reason for the death.**

It is never too late for friends and family to express their feelings about a loss. Nor is there ever a time when that baby should be forgotten.

"The most important role for a person is to hurt with others," one father said. "It is a tough role."

Responding To Grieving Families

WHAT TO SAY
"I'm sad for you."
"How are you doing with all this?"
"This must be hard for you."
"What can I do for you?"
"I'm sorry."
"I'm here, and I want to listen."

WHAT NOT TO SAY
"You're young, you can have others."
"You have an angel in heaven."
"This happened for the best."
"Better for this to happen now before you knew the baby."
"There was something wrong with the baby anyway."
Call the baby a "fetus" or "it."

HOW FRIENDS AND FAMILY CAN HELP
Listen
Touch
Cry with the family
Offer to furnish a meal, to clean the house, do the laundry,
   drive the car pool, etc.
Attend the funeral
Provide an evening of child care
Remember them on their baby's due date, birthday, and
   death day anniversaries.
Never forget

REMEMBRANCES THAT CAN BE GIVEN TO THE FAMILY
Baby ring
Planter/flowers in a baby vase
Original poem
Tree or rose bush as a living memorial
Donation to a memorial fund
Needlework

Parents often find themselves having to respond to well-intentioned
but painful comments. Many find it helpful to respond to the person's

effort to comfort rather than to the exact words. Among possible responses are:

"Thank you for thinking of us in our time of sorrow."

"It is nice to know you are thinking of us."

Other parents respond by squeezing the person's hand or by giving a hug.

If parents feel they must disagree with a hurtful comment, these words might help:

"What you are saying hurts me, rather than helps me. I don't think of my baby's death in that way."

"That isn't how I feel about it."

"A lot of people believe that, but I don't find it comforting."

"I used to think that way, too, before my baby died, but I don't any more."

Some parents find themselves supporting people around them including friends, relatives, and other children in the family.

One mother felt she had to seek approval from grandparents, sisters, and brothers for the funeral arrangements she and her husband wanted. "I think it is important to try to have the strength to do what you want to do despite what other people say," she said. "They are not the ones who have to live with the decisions that are made."

Parents also can show that they feel comfortable with others showing their feelings about the loss. Parents may need to say, "It is OK if you cry. I am comforted by your tears."

As time goes by, parents often find their support dwindling. It may seem that their loved ones have forgotten about their baby. It is not that these people do not care. Most people will continue to offer their support if they know it is needed.

CHAPTER 10

"Watching a child, you think
this is the way we really should be.
I think observing my children
was as much therapy as crying."

INVOLVING CHILDREN

*"I shared the pregnancy
and the death with our children."*

It seemed natural to Mary and Steve to have their children as involved in Jesse's death as they would have been in his life.

"When the kids came, I told the nurse to bring the baby in," Mary said. "It just came naturally. I shared the pregnancy all the way with the children and I would also share this. If I had to share death, this is what I knew I would do."

Rachelle, then five, and Abram, then two, held Jesse and rocked his cradle. "I don't think Chelle even noticed he was too small. He was a baby. Chelle was just intrigued there was a baby her size," Mary said. Abram played "High Five" with the one-pound, two-and-a-half-ounce baby's tiny hands.

Jesse was in Rachelle's arms when he died peacefully, the day after he was born. His premature, Cesarean birth was necessary to save Mary's life.

"The baby was born beautiful, healthy, complete. They told me he would only live two hours, but he survived 24 hours," she said. "Now that I look back on it, I am so wonderfully grateful because the children had a chance to meet their brother. That was so special."

Having the children see and hold Jesse made it easier to explain to them why he died, Mary said. "I knew later that I would get questions, and I wanted real answers they could relate to."

The couple had no set plan for involving the children. "A lot of things we let them do were things that I had not socially seen done before, but it was right for me," Mary said. "It was definitely right for me. I felt I was going on instinct."

Abram and Rachelle were the first children ever allowed in the nursery of the hospital where Jesse was born and died.

The Nelsons, who were new to the community, said they needed to have their children with them. They were the closest relatives - and friends - they had in the area.

The children attended the funeral, although their ability to sit still varied. Rachelle watched, but "Abe went down right next to the casket. He took his car and drove the car over the casket," Mary said. "I thought this was strange, irreverent, not proper. But then I thought, 'This is a child. This is his way of coming in contact with what is going on.'"

Rachelle, because of her age, was better able to understand death than Abram. "When we went back to the hospital for a checkup, Abe would ask if we are going to pick up Jesse," Mary said.

Steve believes he has learned much from watching his children grieve and go on with their lives. "It is almost as if they have taught me to enjoy things again." While he reacted to things because of his prior experience, the children were more innocent in emotions and behavior. "Watching a child, you think this is the way we really should be. I think observing my children was as much therapy as crying."

Mary was startled at first when her children began playing games of death and funerals. "They started playing that their dolls were dying and they had funerals and burials. Dolls died. Cars died. Pretend horses died. Coloring book people died. Mother died."

While it bothered her, she "had a feeling this was their way of expressing their grief. I could handle everything dying until it came to me. I thought, 'Are my kids foretelling the future? Do they know something I don't know? Or, do they wish something? Once they played that Mother died, nothing had to die any more.'"

Because of a threatened miscarriage early in the pregnancy, the couple was concerned about how the children would feel about Jesse and his death. Mary started to hemorrhage while Rachelle was sitting on her lap. "She saw the blood on me. In the next days, when I tried to hold her, she wouldn't sit on my lap. She felt it was her fault."

The problem was resolved by having Mary's nurse-midwife talk to Rachelle. "From that day on, she sat on my lap and does today."

Two years later, Abram and Rachelle "will happen to think about their little brother and be sad," Steve said. "They really can't put it into words. They're just sad."

EXPLAINING DEATH
TO CHILDREN

When a baby dies, children are touched, just as their parents are. They may not know what death is — or have the ability to understand it. But children often feel the tension and sadness when there is a loss in the family. They see their parents anxious and upset. Their normal routine is disrupted. They are separated from their mother while she is in the hospital.

It is natural for parents to want to protect their children from sadness, but children need to learn about the death. The way parents choose to explain the loss, however, is influenced by their past experience and attitudes.

One family takes their toddler to visit his brother's grave at the cemetery. "He relates the cemetery as being a fun thing." his mother said. "A death and a cemetery don't have to be scary. I enjoy going out there."

It may be particularly tempting to avoid telling a child about a miscarriage since the child saw no visible signs of a pregnancy or baby. But if parents think back to when their children were newborns they probably can remember when these tiny babies were able to pick up their tension. The same is true with a death in the family. Even the youngest child picks up on the loss, feels the strain, and senses if something is being withheld.

Children need to be told the truth, simply and honestly. It not only helps children and parents accept the reality, it also builds trust between parent and child. Parents can explain death to children by using these words from *How Do We Tell The Children?* by Dan Schaefer and Christine Lyons:

• Sometimes when a baby is just starting to grow, something happens that makes it stop. We don't know what it was; it wasn't anything anyone did.

- Sometimes something makes a baby die before it is born. We're not sure why, but it's nothing anybody did or didn't do.

- Sometimes with little babies something makes their bodies stop working. It's nothing anybody did or forgot to do. Doctors are not sure why it happens.

Parents must not tell children that the baby is "sleeping," "on a trip," or "lost." These words may be convenient, but they could frighten the child.

Children react to deaths as individually as do adults. It is as normal for one child to be curious and repeatedly asking questions as it is for another youngster to refuse to talk about it. Parents should be prepared to answer the same questions over and over again. For children, once is not enough for many topics, including this one.

Sometimes parents are taken off guard by the things their children say. Some children talk frankly about the death with anyone they meet. "I had a brother and sister, Jay and Jody, but they died," a mother recalled her little boy saying after her twins died. "He felt much more comfortable talking about it than other people did."

Children's grief can be shortlived, too. They may be crying one moment and playing the next.

Ability to understand death will depend a great deal on age. Generally, children age five and younger fear abandonment by or harm to their mother. They feel that death is not final but is temporary like sleep. They also believe they can cause it to happen.

From age five to nine, children may understand it is final but not believe it happens to everybody. At age nine and older, children are able to accept the inevitability of death and some of its causes. Older children may grieve in a more adult way.

Children often have mixed feelings about the arrival of a new baby. Younger children's thoughts center around themselves. If they have had negative feelings about a new baby or their mother, and something goes wrong, they may feel the death was their fault. This guilt needs to be anticipated since children may not be able to express it. They need to be told, perhaps over and over again, that they did nothing to hurt the baby, that thoughts and words do not make babies die.

It is important to encourage, but not force, children to talk about how they feel soon after the loss. Some children may not be ready right away, but their feelings may surface later in dreams, fantasies, or play. Although it may disturb parents to see their children playing death, it is their way of working out and resolving their grief.

One couple used a toy spaceman to explain their baby's stillbirth. They told their children the spaceman's lifeline was similar to the baby's umbilical cord. If the lifeline got tangled, the spaceman could not breathe. Similarly, the baby died when his lifeline became tangled. The children often played the spaceman died in this way.

Parents may wonder how involved their youngsters should be in seeing the baby and attending the funeral. This will vary with their beliefs, but many specialists in child development believe that if children are old enough to say hello, they are old enough to say good-bye.

One family found that having the children hold their premature baby before he died offered them a chance to love him and get to know him. That built a strong bond and a basis for questions and remembrances after his death.

Some families have found the funeral a way of facing the death and bringing the family closer together. Since children are part of happy events, they can also be part of sad times. Parents should prepare children for what will happen and what they will see.

While parents are the best judge of what their children are ready for, it may help to ask them. Parents also can ask a *Resolve Through Sharing* counselor or other helping professional for their ideas. No matter what parents decide, it is the best decision for them at the time.

Children may react to the loss and the stress in the family by regressing in toilet training and sleeping all night. They may seek more attention, become loud and aggressive, or show less interest in school. Gentle encouragement and reassurances of love can help return behavior to normal.

It may not always be easy for parents to give that reassurance. Parenting and grieving are difficult to do at the same time. Both take a great deal of energy. When grieving, parents become irritable. They feel overpowering dependency needs of their own. The stress of day-to-day needs of children, particularly young ones, can seem an unbearable addition to a load that already is overwhelming.

Parents sometimes get angry at their living children because they are alive. Said one mother about her son, "He was born with life on a silver plate."

Children, too, may see parents acting differently and feel threatened. They may feel they lost not only a sibling but their mother and father as well.

One way for parents to lessen the tension is to get away for short breaks without their children. Then, when they return, they may be better able to give the children what they need - assurance of love, honesty, and the knowledge that nothing is kept from them.

Most important, a hug can lessen the pain of bad news and give a feeling of security and safety.

CHAPTER 11

"We hurt twice . . . we hurt for
our children because they are our children.
Plus, we hurt for the grandchild
who died."

GRANDPARENTS' GRIEF

"You want to take the hurt on yourself."

Dorothy and Bob remember the thrill when their daughter called to say they had a granddaughter.

They hoped this beautiful baby would help their daughter, Pat, and her husband, Dan, get over the loss of Benjamin nearly one-and-a-half years earlier.

"She called from the hospital after having Tricia and was so excited," Dorothy recalled.

"Twelve hours later - at six o'clock in the morning - Danny called us all choked up. He said, 'Mom, Tricia's been put in intensive care. It's an instant replay. She's starting to show symptoms already.'"

"Pat just went into shock," Dorothy said, adding she and her husband know about grief both as grandparents and parents. "We lost a child, too . . . our fifth one. According to our doctor, it was an imperfect fetus that should have been aborted. He lived six months."

The couple relived their pain through the deaths of Benjamin and Tricia. "It all came back to us," Bob said. Added Dorothy, "It is a deep pain. That is how I felt." The loss of a grandchild is in sharp contrast with grandparents' expectations. "As a grandparent, you are really excited when you first know that they are expecting. It increases as you are waiting. When the baby is born, you are just so thrilled."

When the baby dies, the pain is doubly severe for grandparents, she said. They not only feel for the grandchild but for their own children as well. And, there is so little they can do. "You want to take away all the hurt and take it on yourself, which is impossible. All you can do is stand by and be as comforting and supportive as you can."

Both Benjamin and Tricia appeared normal at birth. But within two months each had died of a rare and little understood blood disorder.

Pat and Dan never got to take Benjamin home from the hospital. "We only saw him once through the nursery window. He was kind of fat in the face," Bob said.

Tricia came home from the hospital but returned for blood tests every three days. The newborn fought against those tests as best she could. "As little as she was, she would clench her finger and pull her hand back," Dorothy said, adding, "She was pretty, just so pretty."

Bob remembers going to stay with Pat and Dan for a time, to help with the other children. "When I went up there to stay in the house when Tricia was sick, Pat answered the door and said, 'Did you come to see Tricia for the last time?' Holy smoke."

The decision to keep Tricia at home showed a great strength, Dorothy said. "They held that little girl between them until the end."

Tricia's condition was totally unexpected. Everyone, including doctors, thought Benjamin's problems would not repeat themselves. "Pat was apprehensive all nine months of her pregnancy with Tricia," her mother said. "She never had any problems. 'I kept saying God has given you a beautiful baby.' Those words just haunt me."

Dorothy and Bob, as grandparents, went through an intense grief. "The one I feel sorry for is Dorothy. I think it is harder on a woman. She carries that baby for all those months," Bob said. Dorothy was diagnosed as having cancer of the pancreas six weeks after Tricia died. "I think it made Dorothy ill," Bob said. Dorothy agreed, "I still think it triggered cancer in me."

Dorothy and Bob believe grandparents have limited roles in this kind of loss. They should be there to listen.

"We sat there night after night, but what we did was just offer physical comforts. We listened quietly and just poured out our strength to them," Dorothy said. "The main thing we tried to tell Patty and Dan was to rid themselves of any personal guilt."

While they offered support, Bob said they did not try to make decisions for Dan and Pat. "As grandparents, you have to sit until you are asked. You can offer mild suggestions, but not until you really are asked."

DOUBLE HURT . . .
FOR THEIR CHILDREN AND
FOR THEIR GRANDCHILD

Most grandparents have vivid memories of seeing their son or daughter hurt often as children. They remember swooping them up in their arms and kissing the owie, somehow making the hurt go away.

The pain their child feels after losing a baby cannot just be hugged away. The loss may cause a pain deeper than even the grandparents have experienced before. Their children's emptiness and loneliness may make grandparents feel frustrated and powerless to do anything to help the ones they love. "You want to take away the hurt and take it on yourself, which is impossible," a grandmother said sadly.

The pain grandparents feel about the loss is compounded by the feelings they have for their own child. "We hurt twice," another grandmother shared. "We hurt for our children because they are our children. Plus, we hurt for the grandchild who died."

Part of the difficulty for grandparents is they never really stopped being a mommy or daddy. The child may be grown now - old enough to have a baby - but the instinct to protect and to make him or her feel better cannot be turned off.

"When your kids are little, you do everything for them," expressed a grandmother. "When they grow up and something like this happens, you'd like to do something, but there isn't a lot you can do. You just let them know you feel sorry for them and you are hurting. When they're small and hurt their knee, you can kiss it and bandage it up and it's all better in their world. Things like this, you can't."

Grandparents' pain is affected by their expectations. Grandparents make plans for the infant just the way parents do. They wonder if the baby will resemble their side of the family and if the grandchild will get into the same kinds of mischief their own youngster did.

Grandparents' dreams also are shattered, yet this loss may be less apparent to others. "Neighbors and friends for days called us Grandpa and Grandma, and then they didn't know what to call us," a grandfather said.

Parents, so wrapped up in their own grief, may not recognize the pain the grandparents are feeling. "I don't think I had the strength at the time to look at my mother and ask, 'How are you doing?'" a father recalled. "I was too concerned about how I was doing and not how she would handle it."

Grief may be even more troublesome if it is long distance. Grandparents have expressed the need to see or visualize what is going on with their children when they live in another community. Telephone calls and letters can be a poor substitution, especially when the child sounds so sad and they are not close enough to do anything for him or her.

The sets of grandparents may fear intruding on each other's territory. "They have two very different sets of parents tugging over them," a grandfather explained. "I am sure one set of parents sees the other parents and says, 'Let's wait until later.'"

Grandparents also go through the four phases of mourning for a loss. But they have some special concerns. Some search for a cause for the loss and often blame themselves, thinking their genes or chromosomes may have caused the death. "It's really difficult for me, too. I am the mother of 11 children, and, in our family, we've always had babies," a grandmother said. "There are not too many miscarriages, stillbirths, or anything."

Some grandparents may inadvertently blame the parents for the loss, saying such things as:

"We thought you got pregnant too soon."

"Maybe you shouldn't have been working so hard."

"I knew all that running while you were pregnant wasn't good for the baby."

"I told you you weren't eating right or taking care of yourself."

One of the reasons this time is so difficult for grandparents is that parents' emotions are volatile. It is not unusual for a parent to lash out at a grandparent for something said.

Grandparents need to think before making comments that could add guilt and pain to parents at a stressful time. These comments might cause a rift, just when their children need the most comfort.

Grandparents may be angry about the loss, feeling their children should have done something they felt was important during the pregnancy. They may be angry, too, at the doctor for not saving the baby. Some grandparents even feel angry that they are alive and their grandchild is not. This feeling was expressed in Susan Borg's and Judith Lasker's book *When Pregnancy Fails.* "I'll never forget having to bury my grandchild. I felt it should have been me in that grave, not him. The children and grandchildren are supposed to bury old people, not the other way around."

Both generations have talked about a need many grandparents have to take charge in their children's lives at the time of a loss. But most agreed the best role is a supportive one.

"I am a very outgoing person," a grandfather explained. "It is easy for me to take the reins and go at it. But these are not our decisions to make. Certain things have to be done by the parents together."

It is tempting for grandparents to make decisions for their children, such as funeral plans or putting away the infant's toys and clothing. The grandparents do so, thinking they are saving their children pain. But parents often said they later regretted it. Some were even upset. Putting away the baby's things is an important release for parents' feelings, and arranging the funeral the way they want is an important gift the parents can give to their baby.

A grandparent can be a guide, however, without taking charge. Some parents are eager to see and hold the baby. Others feel they should not, even if they would like to. A grandparent cradling the child may give parents "permission" to do so. Not every parent or grandparent wants to hold or see the baby. Those who have, however, often are comforted by it. The moments together are treasured.

Parents also have talked about the help their own parents gave by being there. "She was here. She stayed with me, but she also knew when to leave me alone," a mother, whose twins died, remembered. "I had a couple of friends come to see me who had lost children. When they came, she left us alone for a few minutes. She realized that I needed her there, but I also needed to be alone with my husband and my friends."

Another mother talked about her father who "was there at the right time. He didn't say a word. He just looked at my husband, put his arms around him, and hugged him. My husband broke into tears. I had never seen him cry. It was a real hard cry. It was like he needed the support of a man to understand and hold him without words."

There are other ways for grandparents to provide support. One couple, who had two losses, was touched by the grandfather's desire to help bury their second son. Grandparents also can include the baby who died in conversations and in their count of grandchildren. This alleviates the fear parents have that their infant will be forgotten, somehow erased from the memories of the family.

The loss may be especially troubling for grandparents who are expecting another grandchild soon after the death. They may say things they regret later as they alternate from happiness for one child and sadness for another. "I couldn't believe it when my father said to my sister, 'Now there is another cradle available if you have twins.' I was just in shock," a father said. "I did not know what to do."

The grandparents' role is important because they always have influence over their children no matter how old the children become. Still, they must recognize their child's need to make it through this experience in his or her own way.

Grandparents must always keep room in their heart for memories of the grandchild who has died just as they do for each living grandchild.

Dear Grandma and Grandpa,

My mom and dad are very sad, and I know you are too. I've heard your cries, and I just wish that I could comfort you.

You're asking *why* I had to die. Wishing it were you? You say, "you've lived, I never did, why *me* instead of you?"

Oh, Grandpa, how I'll miss your songs and rides upon your knee. Grandma, I look at you and I know how special my smile to you would be.

I have one small request I hope you'll do for me. It's a gift for mom and dad, given in love from you and me.

Please, kiss my mom, hug my dad, let your tears mingle as one. Listen to them as they talk about the person I would have become. Circle them in your arms, and keep on holding tight. Having your support and love will help them make it through silent nights.

I'm smiling at you through my tears, sleepy in your arms of love. So, I'll sadly say good night to you, from my bed in heaven above.

Hugs and kisses,
Your Grandchild.

from Jessica
to her grandparents,
Armella and Hank Rataj

KATHIE MAYO

CHAPTER 12

*"Helping bereaved parents find
their inner strength in order to deal
with a pregnancy loss is sometimes
painful, sometimes exhausting."*

THE ONE-TO-ONE HELPING RELATIONSHIP

HELPING PARENTS FIND THEIR INNER STRENGTH

Carolyn Smiley, an experienced labor and delivery nurse, remembers the silence in the room while labor was induced for a woman whose baby had died in utero. "No one said anything. No one talked to the mom. I didn't know what to say. I was afraid I might say something to make her feel worse . . . so I didn't say anything. I didn't know that just sitting in the room with the mom would help her."

While working with families with high-risk pregnancies, Smiley became acutely aware of their needs and that more could be done for them. She then decided she needed to learn what to say, needed to find ways to help mothers and fathers who had suffered a loss.

Her "feeling of helplessness" slowly dissipated as she gleaned information from reading whatever she could find about pregnancy loss and grief, observed what other professionals were doing to help bereaved families, and tried to help families herself.

She has found that her experiences with families have contributed the most to her understanding of pregnancy loss, grief, and healing. "I learn something from one family that may be helpful for others."

It has been "a growing process and a long process," Smiley said. "There were times when I had to do what I knew would help parents, no matter what other people thought, such as photograph the child and offer parents time to spend with their dead child."

Although it has taken time, she believes the knowledge she has gained in order to assess grief and individual needs has made it possible for her to give the individualized care parents need. She has learned to be selective in offering options and not to force any of them on the families. She also has learned to give parents time to make their decisions.

"Sometimes parents are so overwhelmed," Smiley said, "that I give information to them bit by bit, as they can handle it. I don't push them, but I let them know that they need to make decisions. I might tell them 'You are caring for this child by making these decisions.'"

Smiley believes the one-to-one helper has two roles:

• to be the primary contact who helps the family, during and after the hospital stay, cope with the loss and integrate it into their lives

• to educate other professionals so they, too, can understand the needs of and help families who have suffered a pregnancy loss.

Being a one-to-one helper is not easy according to Smiley. "Helping bereaved parents find their inner strength in order to deal with a pregnancy loss is sometimes painful, sometimes exhausting. Parents in shock may not be able to tell you if you are helping them or not. But one-to-one helpers should feel good about what they do because they probably are helping and because they care enough to try to help."

THE ONE-TO-ONE HELPER

Staffs of hospitals and clinics today like to think of themselves as providing family-centered obstetrics care. The job is easy when the result is a happy, healthy baby. However, when a loss occurs through miscarriage, ectopic pregnancy, stillbirth or newborn death, the expectations of family and staff suddenly are unfullfilled. All are in crisis.

Health professionals may find themselves at a loss about what to do. By their actions — usually inadvertent — they can make these families feel that their needs are less important than those of parents whose baby was born healthy.

"When other mothers delivered their babies," one mother recalled, "it seemed like the staff was eager to be with them. When our son was stillborn, our doctor barely stuck his head in the door after the delivery. Even the nurses seemed to stay away. We felt like they wanted no part of us."

Faced with a sudden and often unexpected loss, family members are unsure of what they should do. They may feel intimidated by the hospital setting, the staff, and any medical procedures occurring to the mother and baby.

What families need at this time is someone who can help them through this vulnerable period. A professional working in the hospital or clinic should develop what we call the one-to-one helping relationship. The one-to-one helper understands grief, assesses a family's bereavement responses, is non-judgmental, and is committed to helping the family.

This person, usually a registered nurse or a social worker, is an advocate for the family throughout the hospital stay and beyond. The role is to listen to the family, anticipate needs, offer options, and generally help the family regain a feeling of control over their lives. All this is done without preconceived notions of how the family should be feeling or acting.

This person also should recognize the importance of eye contact and touch, and accept tears without attempting to stop their flow. Since some individuals take the offer of a handkerchief as an indication that they should stop crying, handkerchiefs or tissues should be accessible but not necessarily offered.

Other potential one-to-one helpers include staff in the emergency room; a nurse in the neonatal nursery, same day surgery, or out-patient clinic; a chaplain; or a laboratory technician.

This one-to-one helper should look at each family as an opportunity for individual growth. By learning from what helped each family, that individual will be able to assist others even more effectively. This helper also should be one who continues to read and learn about the causes of pregnancy loss and its impact on families.

Parents have an important right after their baby has died — the right to make their own decisions. They need to have options, but they should not be rushed or pushed. Because of the shock or numbness they feel in the initial phases of grief, families may need to be offered these options more than once. Professionals walk a fine line between offering choices and making parents feel guilty about not accepting these options. Parents have the right, and not the obligation, to choose these options. The parents' decisions should be respected.

SEEING AND HOLDING THE BABY

The mother and the father should be asked together if they would like to see the baby or, in the case of a very early miscarriage, the tissue. Sharing this experience helps them acknowledge the death and begin grieving together. They may reject the idea initially but decide later that they very much want to see and hold their baby. If they are questioning what to do, a statement such as "other parents have found it helpful to see the baby" gives parents "permission" to do what otherwise might seem odd or distasteful.

"I was shocked when I learned that a friend whose newborn had died had actually held her infant. When we learned our daughter was going to be stillborn, I felt I could never bring myself to even look at her," a mother said. "Luckily a social worker told us other families were comforted by it. If they were, we thought maybe it was OK to see her. Once she was brought in, wrapped in a blanket, I felt it was right. Once I held her, I felt like I never wanted to let her go."

Parents do need to be prepared for seeing the baby. In an early miscarriage, they should be told what the tissue will look like or how the baby appears. The baby or the tissue should be handled with care and dignity.

In a later loss parents also need to be told how the baby looks. Parents can be told that the baby's skin is red and shiny and peeling, rather than macerated; that darkened areas of the head are a result of pushing during labor. Any other unusual characteristics should be described.

The person bringing the baby to the parents has a wonderful opportunity to be a role model for parents. When a baby is carried and treated as one who is alive, it shows the caregiver's respect for this life. Holding the baby close, touching a hand or cheek, and talking with the baby give parents the message that it is OK for them to do so. It also is important to help the parents explore the baby's body as they desire. Pointing out pretty features or features that resemble the parents helps them feel the baby is theirs.

TAKING PHOTOGRAPHS

Photographs should be routinely taken and kept on file even if parents say they do not want them. Often, parents decide later that they do want them. The opportunity to take pictures will never come again.

When photographs are taken, a ribbon or hat can be strategically placed to cover defects. Different views should be taken, including close-ups of special features (e.g., hands). At least one photograph should be taken of the baby nude so that parents have a chance to see the baby that way, should they wish to do so.

Pictures that include a pretty blanket, baby toy, or fresh or silk flowers provide better photographic memories. Parents also may appreciate a family photo which includes surviving siblings.

Photos taken with a 35 mm camera are ideal. Instant photos tend to fade over time; if parents have only instant photos, they should be encouraged to have negatives made from them.

PROVIDING TIME FOR PARENTING

Parents may want time alone with their baby. They may need several hours to say good-bye and may need to see their baby several times before being taken to the funeral home. This time is their right. *It is the only parenting time they will have with their child.*

Notifying The Clergy

Support from the clergy should be offered all parents. They may wish to see their own pastor or rabbi, a hospital chaplain, or none at all. Clergy can say a blessing or baptize the baby or provide ongoing psychological and spiritual support.

Offering Blessing/Baptism

Families who experience a miscarriage or stillbirth might choose a blessing said in memory of the baby.

Baptism should only be done in accordance with the parents' wishes since some families do not believe in baptism and others believe in adult baptism.

Making Final Arrangements

Choosing a funeral home and director is difficult for parents who have never experienced a loss in their family. A list of local funeral directors and approximate cost of infant funerals is helpful. The one-to-one helper should notify the funeral director as soon as possible. If notification is not given until 12 to 48 hours after the death, the family may inadvertently be caused a great deal of anxiety because they have not heard from the funeral director.

The funeral can be a simple graveside service with a few family and friends or a funeral service with a visitation. It is important that parents know that what they choose need not depend on the size or age of their baby.

"We have never had a death in our family. My parents and grandparents are still living. When Michael died, we had no idea how to go about planning a funeral and even if we wanted one at all," a father said. "My first inclination was to make all the arrangements so my wife would not have to deal with it. The nurse helped us realize that this was a task we should plan together. She helped guide us through it."

Transporting The Baby

Driving the baby to the funeral home not only reduces costs for those living far from the hospital but also gives parents time to be with their baby. Parents should be given details of transporting the baby themselves and then time to decide if they wish to do this. Grandparents, family members, or a pastor sometimes are willing to help by transporting the baby to the funeral home.

EXPLAINING AUTOPSY

An autopsy or genetic studies should be discussed with parents, depending upon the physician's recommendations. Parents need to be told honestly what could be gained by these procedures, that they sometimes — but not always — provide information in determining the cause of the loss and for counseling future pregancies. Most important, the parents need to be reassured that their baby's body is treated with dignity and to be told whether incisions will show should the parents want an open casket.

PRESERVING MEMORIES

Although limited, memories are important because they help the parents come to terms with the loss of their baby. Footprints, handprints, pictures, a lock of hair, and other mementos help bring reality to the life of the baby. Anything used in caring for the baby while in the hospital, be it a brush, baby lotion or powder, should be given to the parents. The blanket in which the baby was wrapped should remain unwashed and be put in a sealed plastic bag. "I opened the plastic bag that had Lisa's blanket and its smell made me feel like she was still a part of us," explained a mother. "This was her blanket. It touched her body. She was real."

RAISING STAFF AWARENESS

Caring for a family in grief requires consistency in care. Bereaved parents should not encounter staff or personnel who do not know their baby has died. Marking the door with a special card or sticker, labeling charts on the outside, and informing the family's primary physician/midwife, pediatrician, or childbirth educator is a courtesy to both the family and their caregiver.

It is not just the medical staff, nurses, social workers, and chaplains who need to understand the grief process. Ancillary staff who come in contact with grieving families, such as housekeeping, IV therapy, maintenance, dietary, and the laboratory, should receive inservice in giving sensitive responses to bereaved parents.

DISCUSSING THE GRIEF PROCESS

As much as parents may wish to get away from the hospital, where their loss occurred, it may be difficult for them. They are leaving a supportive and caring staff to face the unknown response of family and friends. Prior to discharge, they need information about:

- how long grief lasts
- talking with their other children about death
- how men and women often grieve differently
- body changes mothers will experience and how to care for themselves after a loss
- sexuality after a loss
- getting pregnant again
- the reactions of family and friends.

A lending library and a bibliography of available literature are very helpful to parents who are interested in reading more about a loss. It is not enough, however, to just hand parents reading material. Parents need to be told in advance how they may be affected.

EXPLAINING SUPPORT GROUPS

If a parent support group is available, parents should be informed about the group and its next meeting time and place. Attending the first meeting is sometimes very difficult for parents. The one-to-one helper can provide an important service by going to the first meeting with them. Parents may need time to decide if they wish to attend. Only about ten percent of families who experience a loss actually come to these meetings.

PROVIDING FOLLOW UP

The one-to-one helper should contact parents by telephone in the weeks after discharge to answer their questions, see how they are doing, and talk about how they are feeling. When making the call, it is important to assess the family's physiological, emotional, and social grief response. Sometimes a question about how the partner or the children are doing may open the discussion. These follow-up calls show care and concern and let parents know there is a place to turn for support if it is needed. These calls are especially important on special dates — when the baby was due, the anniversary of the loss and when the couple learned of the pregnancy.

PLANNING A GRIEF CONFERENCE

A grief conference is an important opportunity for parents to talk with their physician, their advocate, and others they wish present to discuss the events and details of the loss. Autopsy and genetic studies can be discussed. If these were not done, a review of what is known about the loss is helpful. Parents should be encouraged to ask questions. Often, they are more interested in suggestions for helping themselves through their grief than in learning the technical causes of the loss. Many parents just need to go over the events of the loss with staff members who were present. The grief conference is also an opportunity for the staff to assess how the mother and father are doing as individuals and as a couple.

Some families may need therapy in helping them work through their grief. Professionals working in a one-to-one helping relationship need to be aware of the differences between uncomplicated grief and complicated grief. They should develop a list of clinical psychologists, psychiatrists, or other therapists for bereaved families who need them.

The primary role of the one-to-one helper is to slow down the system in order to give parents the time they need to say good-bye and to make the decisions that feel right to them.

Checklists for the one-to-one helper to assure continuity and consistency in care for all bereaved families appear on pages 128-132.

CHAPTER 13

"I am more sensitive to how other events affect these families beyond what they are saying and what they are sharing with me."

THE PHYSICIAN'S RESPONSE

MORE THAN "JUST A MISCARRIAGE"

In his early years of practice, Dr. Ted Peck considered miscarriage to be a "setback" but not a tremendous loss to his patients. Peck, a board-certified perinatologist who also has a general obstetrics practice, assumed parents did not have the intense grief for an early pregnancy loss as they did when a baby died through stillbirth or as a newborn. He knew that statistics, after all, favored women who, once or twice, had had a miscarriage. Most would be able to have a full-term baby.

But his view has changed tremendously, in great part because of his association with Resolve Through Sharing at La Crosse Lutheran Hospital. Peck now believes he "missed the psychological boat" about how deeply a miscarriage can affect parents.

He began changing his view when he found himself the only person on the Resolve Through Sharing *organizing committee* fighting to limit the program to parents who had experienced stillbirth or newborn deaths. He felt that including those who had experienced a miscarriage or an ectopic pregnancy would not only be unnecessary but would stretch the program staff to the limit.

"Fortunately, I was overruled," he said. "I am glad that they were smarter than I was."

After that experience Peck began reading more about miscarriage losses and listening to the comments his patients made. He began routinely using ultrasound early in pregnancies for women who had had a prior miscarriage. This examination, in most cases, can relieve fears because a baby's chances for survival are 90 to 95 percent if a heartbeat can be seen on the ultrasound.

The final evidence needed to change his belief about miscarriage occurred while doing an ultrasound for a woman in her first trimester of pregnancy. The woman, who had had a previous miscarriage, appeared happy and content. He remembers making the comment, "I'll bet you are worried about having another miscarriage."

At that point the woman broke down and cried. She then told him how worried and upset she was about the possibility of another miscarriage and how she still grieved for her baby who died.

"What hit me was that this woman seemed as happy and comfortable and satisfied as many other pregnant women, but underneath that smiling face was terrible turmoil and anxiety because of the previous miscarriage. It struck me that I had been looking at a lot of smiling faces, yet I had never really gotten under the surface."

While Peck always considered himself sensitive to the needs of his patients, that experience and many others like it have vastly increased his awareness.

"It also has made me more sensitive to the fact that there are many things in a person's life that can cause similar grief. A woman who has an infertility problem may grieve every time she menstruates. A parent who has a child born with a defect, even a minor one, mourns, too.

"I am more sensitive to how other events affect these families beyond what they are saying and what they are sharing with me. This has been proven to me over and over again as I care for families who have had a miscarriage, ectopic pregnancy, stillbirth, or newborn death."

A Physician Is Trained
To Save - Not Lose - Lives

Many of us have Norman Rockwell images of the family doctor. In our mind we see a white-haired doctor who treated everyone, from grandparent to baby, for everything. We also remember the magic we believed was contained in the little black bag doctors used to tote to our homes. Today, we still believe the medicine practiced by highly-trained specialists can work miracles — especially for babies. So when we discover no miracles can be performed, we are at a tremendous loss.

Physicians, too, have images of themselves and their fellow practitioners. All of their training, their very role, is geared for preserving life.

When a baby or an adult dies, even the most highly trained and experienced doctor suffers a blow to professional confidence as well as a personal sense of failure. While every doctor realizes intellectually that not everyone will live, the physician — as a human — feels just a bit more vulnerable each time a patient dies.

Families turn to their doctor, seeking support and answers for the loss. Physicians, feeling their own personal loss, must find a way to help families, yet stay professional and able to deal with the other patients in their care.

No two physicians accept losses in the same way. Some have become hardened to these losses and do not show emotions to families. While others can and do show their feelings when working with families.

Physician Response
And Responsibility

Informing parents that their baby has died is the responsibility of physicians, but they often have little training in dealing with the aftermath of infant death. Since they have been taught to suppress their emotions so as not to frighten or upset patients, physicians often mask their grief and personal disappointment with silence, reassurance, or insensitive behavior.

The physician's response can be important in terms of future relationships with the family. Parents want the support of the physician they have trusted through the pregnancy. Their physician's words and actions are replayed constantly as the parents go over and over the events leading to and following the death. Often, decisions about whether the physician will care for the mother during subsequent pregnancies are made in the few moments after the death has occurred.

When parents do not get the support they expect or feel the physician has treated them insensitively, the bad experience is shared with friends and family.

Use Sincere And Simple Gestures

A sincere expression, such as "I'm sorry for your loss," is very comforting to parents. A touch on the arm or an arm around the mother's or father's shoulders also has great meaning. If a parent is crying, it is important to move closer so that individual does not feel isolated. **Long explanations are unnecessary and generally useless.**

One woman remembers the time her doctor visited her in the hospital to explain the uncertainty of her unborn baby's chances to live after birth. "As he left the room, the doctor reached down and squeezed my toes. That simple gesture assured me that I wouldn't be facing the uncertain outcome alone."

Handle With Care And Dignity

Parents appreciate it when physicians call their baby a baby or by name rather than calling their baby a fetus. No matter how young this baby is and how little the world has known of him, the parents still want this child treated with dignity. To the parents this was the long hoped-for baby, not a medical specimen to be pushed aside. As one father said, "If my son had been 16, they wouldn't have put him in a metal bowl."

Any comments the physician makes concerning the baby help parents feel good about that child. Something positive usually can be said about any baby, including one whose body is macerated. The physician can remark about the baby's pretty hair, eyes, hands, or feet.

"I felt that he really did care. When he handed the baby to us the doctor said, 'Here's your son, Joey,'" recalled a mother.

At the moment of loss, parents often do not know what is "appropriate" behavior. Physicians can guide them through these hours and days by giving them choices and then giving them time to make up their mind.

One mother still regrets that her physician did not suggest she hold her miscarried baby or spend any time with him. "The baby was between my legs. Then the doctor put him in a bowl. At least I saw him. I didn't know that it was OK to touch him or hold him. I was in a state of shock," she said.

Don't Add To The Guilt

Parents have complex and intense feelings, including guilt and anger, after they lose their baby. Their physician can help them deal with these powerful emotions by decreasing the load, not adding to it.

Comments such as "You'll just have to be more careful next time" or "You'll just have to come see me earlier next time" can cause pain and send messages to parents that they are to blame for the loss.

Differences in how physicians treat women who deliver healthy babies versus women whose babies die also send messages to parents. The absence of a physician's attention says that these parents are less worthy than parents whose baby lived.

ASSESSING GRIEF

Physicians are responsible for the physical care of their patients, be they parent or child. Yet so much of the health of that mother or father is dependent upon how he or she works through the grief.

Parents need to know that:

• even the strangest thoughts and emotions are normal

• that grief does not last just a few days but can continue for a year or more.

Physicians can be a guide by helping parents express their thoughts and emotions during these hard times. In order to do that, physicians must assess the grief response of the mother and father, as well as those of other children in the family, by observing the family's words, emotional state, facial expressions, body positions, and mental alertness.

It is easy to recognize the initial grief responses of families - tears, staring off into space, or shock. Some parents may become manic.

During these early moments, it is helpful if physicians:

• offer privacy in a comfortable place for the family.

• are patient in asking questions, often several times, because people in shock have difficulty comprehending, responding, and making decisions.

• make sure a friend or relative is called to be a support person and to arrange transportation. Parents should not drive after a shock of this kind. If they protest that they are capable of driving, they may not realize that they are in shock. "I was not that upset by the miscarriage," a mother said, adding later, "I don't know how I got home."

Long explanations to parents in shock are useless. If a parent cannot make eye contact, he or she is unlikely to comprehend what is said.

Later on, the physician can explain:

• the mother may experience physiological changes that ordinarily follow childbirth, such as afterpains and lactation

- it is normal for mothers to feel "aching arms," to be pre-occupied with the baby, to have dreams about the baby, to be irritable, and to have mood swings
- the common differences in the ways mothers and fathers grieve.

  Fathers also tend to want to know:
- more details about why the death occurred
- its chances of happening again.

When one mother talked openly about her miscarriage while her husband refused to talk about it at all, she was particularly pleased when her physician "expressed concern that the father was so quiet and didn't open up and express his feelings."

As time goes on, the couple's grief response should be assessed by looking for sleeping problems, changes in their health, social relationships, and work experiences, and any difficulty in handling their other children. Some indications are not as obvious, such as guilt, anger, or fears about future babies. It may take a little probing below the surface to help parents who have lost a baby to talk about their feelings. Simply saying, "Tell me what you've been feeling," or "Tell me what you've been thinking about since your miscarriage" may open emotions and thoughts.

It is important to recognize that parents may have difficulty handling their other children and may overreact to an illness or behavioral problem their youngsters may have.

At each visit, it is helpful to talk about the grief response, to reassure families that it does take time to heal, and to acknowledge that the father and the mother may have trouble communicating with each other because of the differences in the way they grieve.

Physical examinations for the mother and the father about four months after the loss are very important. Initial support from family and friends may have waned by this time, and signs of difficulty between parents may be present. It is important to schedule this appointment, if possible, during the hours when gynecological, rather than obstetric, patients are seen.

Physicians should be careful in the words they use with families. Parents are extremely offended by the medical term "spontaneous abortion" because the negative connotations of the word "abortion" make them feel tainted at a time when they are vulnerable. The lay term "miscarriage" is more acceptable and clearly understood by parents.

SUGGESTIONS FOR WORKING WITH LOSSES

MISCARRIAGE

- Be aware that most women grieve for a miscarriage, though some grieve little or not at all.
- Be aware that most men want information about miscarriage and what they can do for their partner.
- Use the term "miscarriage" instead of the term "abortion."
- In subsequent pregnancies, acknowledge that parents may fear another miscarriage.
- Use ultrasound to show the parents that the pregnancy is viable.
- Recognize that many women feel guilty about the miscarriage. While you may have told them at the time of the loss that there was nothing they could have done to prevent it, this should be repeated when they are better able to comprehend this information.
- Make a special appointment to meet with parents for a follow-up examination four to six weeks after the loss. This may not be needed physically, but it is another opportunity for them to express their feelings about the loss and about their relationship. It also is a time when they can be told again that the chances of having a healthy baby are excellent even after one or two miscarriages.

ECTOPIC PREGNANCY

- Be sensitive that parents may be mourning for the loss of future pregnancies as well as this one. Help them understand how the ectopic pregnancy has affected their ability to conceive again.
- Recognize that feelings about the loss may be masked for a time while the woman recovers from major surgery and comes to understand what happened to her.

- Be aware that some individuals may not mourn the loss at all but be more upset about changes in their body image.

STILLBIRTH

- Pay special attention to the emotional condition of the mother who may be horrified by carrying a dead baby.
- Help the mother and her partner understand the advantages and disadvantages of waiting for labor to begin spontaneously and of inducing labor after the baby has died.

    ADVANTAGES OF INDUCING LABOR
    - The psychological stress of carrying a baby who has died can be reduced.
    - The shorter the time between death and delivery, the more the baby's features resemble the typical newly-born infant. That may be important to some parents.
    - It is difficult for mothers who know their baby has died to answer questions from friends and relatives.
    - Potential complications of disseminated intravascular coagulation (DIC) may be avoided.
    - Evaluation of the baby is easier and more accurate if born soon after death.

    DISADVANTAGES OF INDUCING LABOR
    - Induction can be medically difficult to do, particularly if the mother's cervix is not ready. This could lead to an unnecessary Cesarean birth.
    - Medications to induce labor can lead to complications.
    - Labor will nearly always begin spontaneously within four weeks if nature is allowed to run its course.

- Offer parents the choice of waiting, if it is possible medically, but tell them that, generally speaking, delivery soon after the baby has died has its advantages over waiting for spontaneous labor. If they cannot make a decision, encourage them to return in a few days to review the advantages and disadvantages.

- Explain to parents that labor of a baby who has died may be shorter in duration and pushing may be less intense than with a live birth. It also may be more difficult to push because the birth means the final end to the idea of having the baby. Once the baby is born, the faint hopes that the infant would still be alive are lost.

- Try to learn the cause of death through any means possible. This is useful for preventing future losses, for giving the parents confidence in subsequent pregnancies, and for informing their other children if the problem could be inherited.

• Recognize that the shock of a stillbirth is intense and will affect the parents deeply throughout future pregnancies. Make opportunities for the parents to express their concerns.

• Be sensitive to the father's feelings and try to involve him in as much of the prenatal care as possible in subsequent pregnancies.

NEWBORN DEATH

• Provide every medical, nursing, and ancillary service available to help care for the baby.

• When, in the physician's professional opinion, the baby's condition has reached the point where death is inevitable, let the parents know that they do have a choice in the care:

> • Continuing as is, including respirators or other monitoring devices.

> • Providing care that seemingly gives the baby comfort - fluids, nutrition, and warmth.

> • Removing life supports and allowing the baby to die in his parents arms, if they wish. The physician should be willing to give his or her opinion about what is best for the baby but should respect the parents' decision.

• Encourage contact between parent and child throughout the baby's life. Involve parents whenever and wherever possible in day-to-day care, such as changing the diaper. This gives parents a greater sense of control and purpose.

SUBSEQUENT PREGNANCIES

• Once it has been determined that the woman had a previous loss, assess the past experiences and the grief response of the woman and her family.

• Pay special attention to the causes that led to the previous loss so parents will be reassured that all that is possible is being done for them.

• Evaluate the baby's condition frequently, doing ultrasound and non-stress tests even if not absolutely necessary medically.

• Ask periodically throughout the pregnancy how the parents are doing.

AUTOPSY

One of the most difficult questions parents have to face after their baby has died is whether to have an autopsy.

They need to understand that an examination of the body after death can sometimes, but not always, provide the reason for the loss. The examination might provide information that could prevent future losses for that family or others. If the information does, indeed, help others, this can add real meaning to the parents' loss.

One mother was touched by a letter she received more than two decades after an autopsy was done on her daughter, who died a few days after birth. "One of the physicians on her case said the information that they had learned from our daughter had helped a baby that week. It really meant a lot to me. It was very nice. He didn't have to take the time to do that."

Some physicians and medical centers recommend autopsies after every death; others are more selective, believing that if the cause is known the study is not needed unless the parents desire it.

When discussing autopsy, physicians should make sure parents understand:

- what is involved in this examination

- their baby will be treated with respect and dignity

- funeral or burial plans need not be delayed nor the family's desire for an open casket be precluded

- preliminary results usually are available within one to two days following the autopsy, while complete results, including microscopic studies, require six weeks to two months; these results should be discussed fully with the family.

GRIEF CONFERENCE - A TIME FOR TALKING

A grief conference should be scheduled about four to eight weeks after a loss, so the family can talk about any concerns they have about their baby's death.

This is a good time for the grief conference because:

- the shock of the loss generally has worn off
- support from other family and friends has likely waned or even ended
- parents may feel completely alone with the pain and uncertainty of their grief
- the relationship between mother and father may be strained by the differences in the way they express their grief.

The conference should be attended by the parents and family members, any physicians, clergy, counselors, and social workers they would like present. Parents should be encouraged to bring a list of questions and concerns. They should be given a copy and explanation of the autopsy and other laboratory or medical reports during (not before) the conference.

This is a time to reassure parents that their grief is normal even if their thoughts and emotions appear strange to them.

Checklists for the physician to assure continuity and consistency in care for all bereaved families appear on pages 133-137.

"When the youngster dies in
their arms that literally
snatches victory from defeat."

A PIECE OF HUMANITY

Dr. J. Michael Hartigan used to have an "incredible sense of failure" when a newborn died. "I desperately do not like to lose a youngster," he said, "but now, when I realize nothing will prevent the baby's death, I give a piece of my humanity."

Hartigan, a neonatalogist with a general pediatrics practice, gives the child back to the parents, "the only people who have anything left to offer the youngster."

He meets with the parents and tells them their baby is dying, that there is nothing medicine or nursing can do. He then gives them choices in the care of their infant: continuing every possible means of prolonging the baby's life; doing the things that seem to give comfort, such as fluids, nutrition, or warmth; or allowing the baby to die in the parents arms.

"At that point, most physicians abdicate responsibility," Hartigan said. "They make parents face the most terrible decision of their lives and then deny them their opinion."

Hartigan, despite concerns early on that he would be sued for making such a suggestion to parents, has found that they appreciate his opinion. "What I say is 'If I were in this situation, here is what would have meaning to me. It is an opinion. You are free to disagree with my opinion. I will abide by your choice not mine.'"

Offering baby and parents time together in these final moments, has changed Hartigan's tremendous feeling of failure. "The amazing thing to me is from that moment on I no longer had this sense of professional inadequacy. When the youngster dies in their arms that literally snatches victory from defeat."

While Hartigan once expected parents would take him into court, he now finds that he and the parents become friends. "It is a thrill when they later call me and say 'We're pregnant.' They are very special. People who can endure this are really my heroes."

CHAPTER 14

*"The funeral is a statement
that there was a life,
that a life was created."*

THE ROLE OF THE FUNERAL DIRECTOR

A FRIEND IN GRIEF

O.J. Fawcett is particularly "touched" as a funeral director when a child dies, although he has not personally experienced the loss of a child.

"We are all more emotionally involved with a child's death than we are with older people. Anyone feels that way. It's a little more draining," he said. The difference is that the death of a child "is not part of the natural way. Normally parents age and go first."

Working with families who have lost a baby requires additional time and sensitivity, Fawcett feels. "There's probably a greater necessity to explain options to the family who has had a loss of an infant. They tend to be younger and have no experience with death and the grieving process."

These families not only need additional information about funeral options, they also need time to make their decisions.

Funeral directors should not suggest hurrying the funeral so the parents can "put it behind them." The loss takes time to resolve. A rushed service will not shorten that time. The service should wait until both parents can participate.

Fawcett believes parents should be as active in the funeral as they wish. They have the right to see, hold, rock, and dress their baby. Their requests should be respected if at all possible.

But parents also should be prepared for their baby's appearance. "Many times the reality of how their baby looks is not as bad as what they might conjure up in their minds." Parents need to be told their baby's body will be at room temperature, not 98.6 degrees, and also will be more rigid than a living infant.

If the baby has had an autopsy, the parents should be told about the incision which can be covered discreetly with gauze. "Not seeing the baby may be really awful for them, but if they don't realize the extent of the incision (for the autopsy), that might be upsetting to them, too."

Fawcett has worked with the Resolve Through Sharing program and other organizations that help grieving families. He has an extensive library of books, pamphlets, films, and other materials on grief and loss that he not only lends to grieving families but also makes available to his community for public education.

Fawcett does not suggest to families what kind of service they should have because needs are so individualized. Nor does he recommend a certain cost.

But he does believe in the importance of some kind of service even for a baby so young he or she might not have been known by many people. Noting the need parents have to talk about their baby who has died, Fawcett said the funeral gives families and friends memories of that short life. "The funeral is a statement that there was a life, that a life was created."

AN OPPORTUNITY
FOR EXPRESSING LOVE

The focus of a funeral director appears to be in caring for the dead, but these professionals really are caring for the living. True, they have a technical expertise in preparing bodies for burial, but their greater role is as a friend in grief, to help families deal with death.

Today, an increasing number of funeral directors recognize how important it is for parents to plan the funeral for their baby themselves. They are beginning to understand that love is not measured by the size of the person or by how long the parents knew their baby. Attachment to and love for a baby is an affair of the heart. That's why parents of a baby who died early in pregnancy may want the same ritual and ceremony as parents whose baby died at birth or shortly after.

Traditionally, funeral directors believed that parents whose child died needed to be taken under their wing, to be protected. Often they thought parents — especially mothers — "couldn't take" the responsibility of making funeral arrangements. Directors felt they knew what parents needed and that was to have the service "over and done with." Their intentions, to spare parents as much pain as possible, were good. Sparing pain, however, was impossible. At best, it only delayed grieving.

The pressure funeral directors feel to protect the parents — and the public — may have come from the common public perception that dead people should look like they are asleep. At any funeral, comments can be heard like, "He looks so natural," "She looks just like she did in life," or "He looks like he could just be asleep."

Knowing the way the public responds at funerals, funeral directors may be torn between wanting to do what they feel is right for the parents and what the parents request. Because the baby who has died in the uterus or the infant who has been in the morgue for several days may not look like the typical newly-born baby, the funeral director may fear a public viewing will offend some persons.

At times the funeral director's well-intentioned desire to give the parents a pretty good-bye clashes with the need the mother and father have:

- to be with their baby
- to face and accept the death as reality.

They may directly or indirectly discourage parents from seeing or spending time with their baby because the infant is imperfect. Many parents have been offended when well-intentioned funeral directors made comments they felt were judgmental, such as:

"I don't think that is a very good idea."

"You wouldn't want to do that."

"Baby has been dead for three days now and has started decomposing."

"I wouldn't recommend it."

"Do it as quickly as you can."

But parents have said over and over again that they did not care how their baby looked. It was more important for them to express their love and have a picture — both mental and photographic — of their child.

Many funeral directors now realize that viewing the baby shortly after death, even if the baby appears deformed, is an important encounter for parents. It helps parents face and accept the reality of the baby's death.

Viewing the baby a second time, after careful attention has been given to restorative embalming procedures, may fulfill more needs of the parents, particularly if they dress the infant in special clothing and blankets they had prepared. They also have the opportunity to look again at the infant's toes, nose, ears, or other features that they might have missed when so upset at the initial viewing. This may be a time to share the baby with siblings and grandparents. It can be a last chance to place a ribbon in the hair or a special locket in the hand, to tuck the blankets gently around the infant as they say good-bye.

Parents should not be pressured to have their baby embalmed. They may be more willing, however, if they understand that when done with delicate care embalming can stabilize the rapidly deteriorating newborn tissue. No chemical or cosmetic can conceal the reality of death from heartbroken parents, but embalming may give the parents a measure of comfort or a sense of peace.

The funeral director may feel the pressure of public opinion concerning parents who want to have their baby viewed publicly or to rock him or her a last time. One funeral director handled that problem by quietly suggesting guests take a walk for a few minutes until the parents were finished.

Parents have said helpful funeral directors:

- allowed them to design their own funerals
- let them come in and spend time with the baby, rocking, dressing, and holding him or her
- provided a bassinette or cradle for the viewing of the baby
- offered music that was more appropriate for a child's funeral
- provided materials on grieving to help them understand their loss.

A helping relationship can begin when the funeral director visits parents in the hospital. During the time between the death and the release of the baby from the hospital, the funeral director can discuss options with the parents, allowing them time to make decisions best for them.

A checklist for the funeral director to assure continuity and consistency in care for all bereaved families appears on pages 138-139.

CHAPTER 15

"God's was the first
of all hearts to break."

THE ROLE
OF THE CLERGY

LISTENING IS THE
TRUE ROLE OF THE CLERGY

*K*aren and Tom Moe thought they had proof God would
answer their prayers. Two years before their son Brian was born,
Tom's brother and sister-in-law were expecting a child. Tests during the
pregnancy indicated the baby would be born with Spina Bifida.

Moe, who is a minister, and his church began praying for that baby.
When the infant was born normal, we thought "God is good to us."

When the Moes' son was born prematurely and lived just six hours,
the shock was great. "I thought when we started to have problems that
all we would do is pray and God would answer our prayers. When
that didn't happen, I was really thrown for a loss personally.

"Was it something I had done wrong in my life? Were we out of
God's will? Was God angry with me? It doesn't take long for anyone

in life to look for things and start blaming themselves. I was just trying to find a cause for why Brian died."

The experience was a test of his beliefs, Moe said. "All of a sudden I needed answers to my questions. Even your faith collapses in front of you. It was really tough to go back and minister to people and preach on Sunday when I couldn't figure out what happened."

While his faith survived Brian's death, Moe said he does worry about people "who are from marginal spiritual backgrounds, who ask if God is punishing them because of this. This thing could really destroy people. We thought we were really secure in our faith."

The experience changed him professionally as well as personally. Before Brian died, Moe said he "basically, took the approach that I should try and give them answers. I didn't want people to question their faith. I didn't want people to question God for doing these things. That shows weakness in their faith. I wanted to make people strong."

He now realizes, having come through his own loss, "how wrong that was." Since Brian died, Moe has written letters apologizing to others he now believes he counseled incorrectly.

Moe believes it is essential for those whose baby has died to recognize that their loss is unique but their feelings may be common with other parents in similar situations.

"I thought that was the most painful, feeling alone and feeling like nobody knew how I felt. Nobody wanted to talk about our feelings. We were in our own world. We wanted to talk about Brian. We wanted to talk about how much he meant to us.

"It made us feel bad that we had a child and people didn't want to have anything to do with him simply because he had died. We felt like they were rejecting us when they rejected our child."

However, the couple did receive flowers on Brian's fourth birthday. The anonymous gift showed them that somebody out there still remembered him.

There is only one reference in the Bible to Jesus visiting with a grieving family, Moe said. That verse, the shortest in the Bible, says: "Jesus wept." The Moes have spent the years since Brian's death with other couples whose child has died. Listening to others, particularly in their time of pain, is the true role of a minister, according to Moe.

Viewing God's Role In The Death And The Healing

Whena baby dies, families struggle with some terrible questions.

"Was it God's will for the baby to die?"

"Was it God's plan?"

"What did I do to cause God to punish me?"

"Why didn't God take me instead?"

The death can lead to a loss of faith, a bitterness or an anger towards everyone - including God.

A minister, priest, or rabbi can be an important part of the team caring for families at a time of loss, especially if they are knowledgeable about grief. In many communities clergy are the only professionals available 24 hours a day when the family needs them most.

Clergy may be the only professionals who see families regularly - often week to week. Observant priests, rabbis, or ministers have the opportunity to assess how families are dealing with their loss. Members of the clergy can help parents get in touch with the persons who can be of greatest support to them, including others in the congregation who have gone through or are going through a similar kind of loss.

The assistance given by clergy will vary with different religious groups, of course. Some groups believe God preordained everything that happens to us, including deaths. Others see God as causing bad things to happen as punishment. When these views are held, the meaning of the loss is best interpreted by clergy of that individual religion or denomination, especially when these religious persons are part of a team of other helping professionals.

"GOD'S WAS THE FIRST OF ALL HEARTS TO BREAK."

Many others, however, view God as suffering with each loss. It is for these people that the bulk of this chapter is written.

The Rev. William Sloane Coffin, Jr., senior minister of Riverside Church in New York City, talked about this view of God after his 24-year-old son died when the car in which he was driving went into the Boston Harbor.

God does not have his "finger on triggers, his fist around knives, his hands on steering wheels," Coffin wrote in an article about his son's death in *The Lutheran Standard.* "God is against all unnatural deaths. And Christ spent an inordinate amount of time delivering people from paralysis, insanity, leprosy and muteness."

One thing should never be said when someone dies, Coffin said. "'It is the will of God.' Never do we know enough to say that. My consolation lies in knowing that it was *not* the will of God that Alex died; that when the waves closed over the sinking car, God's was the first of all hearts to break."

There is no fairness to the loss, but if families see that God is with them in their sorrow, that the child is in God's hands, they may find comfort in the midst of the tragedy.

A minister, rabbi, or priest does not need to answer for or defend God. God is big enough to withstand anger and feelings of frustration and still love the people expressing those emotions. It is best for clergy to provide presence to parents. Platitudes and "God language" are unnecessary.

Clergy have a special role in working with families who have a baby that is about to or already has died. They can help families realize that they need to celebrate the life, no matter how short it was.

When called to the neonatal nursery to baptize the baby before death, the minister or priest should slow down the process. Rather than feeling a sense of urgency to get the baptism over with, the clergy member can touch the family and baby both emotionally and physically.

It is important to call the baby by name and to comment on the baby's beautiful hair or the color of the baby's eyes. If the clergy member is comfortable, he or she can touch the baby, perhaps taking the infant's hands. This touch is important because, later, the minister can point out to those attending the funeral that this was a real person by saying, "This is an infant that I, too, touched" or "I know how soft this baby was."

Sometimes, parents are unsure if it is right to hold the baby after death. Having their priest, rabbi, or minister hand them the baby often gives them "permission" to hold and cuddle their child.

This involvement touches the family's life because it makes the pastor a *participant* rather than an *observer* in the baby's life.

It may be more difficult for the clergy to touch families in the same way when the loss was through miscarriage. The minister, priest, or rabbi may not have the same tangible experience on which to comment as with stillbirth or newborn death. Still, the religious person's presence can be helpful. She can talk about when the couple first learned about the pregnancy or hopes, dreams or plans for the baby. If the clergy member was not aware the mother had been pregnant, he can talk about the first meeting with the couple or when they wed.

The presence of the clergy represents to many people the presence of God. Being present early on helps the family place the infant in God's care. This spiritual resource gives hope in the midst of trouble.

An important role of the clergy is to help the parents explore any feelings of guilt they may have. The clergy member can help parents sort through their guilt, acknowledge any responsibility, and come to a sense of forgiveness and acceptance.

A rabbi, priest, or minister cannot give an answer for why the loss occurred except to say that we live in a world where bad things happen. Clergy cannot say they understand what families are feeling, because they really do not know how it feels to have *their* loss, even if special persons in their own lives have died. Each death is unique.

The best gift anyone can give is to listen, taking such approaches as:

"I am willing to talk about it with you."

"I am willing to cry with you."

"I am willing to hurt with you."

A clergy member who has had a loss may share this by saying, "I know something of what you are feeling. My baby died 20 years ago."

When clergy see members of their congregations regularly, they should watch these families as time goes on and ask questions like "How are you dealing with your loss?" This gives them the opportunity to open up, if they wish. They can provide parents with long-term access to on-going care and support through their period of grieving.

In this time of crisis, families may need temporary spiritual comfort even if they have no affiliation with a church or denomination.

A checklist for the clergy member to assure continuity and consistency in care for all bereaved families appears on pages 140-141.

CHECKLISTS
ONE-TO-ONE HELPER

MISCARRIAGE OR ECTOPIC PREGNANCY

Notify
- ☐ Pastoral care/clergy
- ☐ Regular obstetrician/nurse-midwife
- ☐ Childbirth educator
- ☐ Funeral director
- ☐ Genetics clinic

☐ Ask question, "Would you like someone with you now?"

Offer to show baby or tissue to
- ☐ Mother
- ☐ Father
- ☐ Grandparents
- ☐ Other family or friends

Offer opportunity to touch or hold baby to
- ☐ Mother
- ☐ Father
- ☐ Grandparents
- ☐ Other family or friends

☐ Offer blessing/baptism

Remembrance of Blessing card
- ☐ Given to parents
- ☐ On file

☐ Discuss Dilatation and Curettage (D&C)

☐ If Rh negative, give RhoGAM

☐ If on maternity unit, offer option to transfer

☐ Flag patient's room as bereaved family

Take photos
- ☐ Given to parents
- ☐ On file

Footprints/handprints
- ☐ Given to parents
- ☐ On file

Give grief packet to
- ☐ Mother
- ☐ Father

Discuss grief process with
- ☐ Mother
- ☐ Father

Discuss differences in grieving between men and women with
- ☐ Mother
- ☐ Father

☐ Provide name/business card of one-to-one helper

☐ Send information on family to person keeping records of losses

☐ Offer information about parent support group

☐ Offer option of another parent calling
- ☐ Accepted
- ☐ Declined

Parent contact _____

☐ Verify telephone number
- ☐ Learn optimal calling time

☐ Follow-up calls

_____

_____

_____

_____

ONE-TO-ONE HELPER

Stillbirth Or Newborn Death

Notify
- ☐ Pastoral care/clergy
- ☐ Communications
- ☐ Regular obstetrician/nurse-midwife
- ☐ Pediatrician
- ☐ Childbirth educator
- ☐ Funeral director

Offer to show baby to
- ☐ Mother
- ☐ Father
- ☐ Grandparents
- ☐ Other family or friends

Offer opportunity to touch or hold baby to
- ☐ Mother
- ☐ Father
- ☐ Grandparents
- ☐ Other family or friends

☐ Arrange for reverse transport of baby to mother's hospital, if applicable

☐ Offer private time with baby

☐ Offer blessing/baptism

Remembrance of Blessing card
- ☐ Given to parents
- ☐ On file

☐ Explain opportunity for donating eyes or other organs

☐ If Rh negative, make RhoGAM assessment

☐ If on maternity unit, offer option to transfer

☐ Flag patient's room as bereaved family

☐ Discuss possibility of autopsy
- ☐ Parents agreed to autopsy
- ☐ Parents declined

☐ Discuss possibility of genetic studies
- ☐ Parents agreed to studies
- ☐ Parents declined

Take photos

☐ Polaroid	☐ 35 mm Photos	☐ Medical photos
☐ Given to parents	☐ Given to parents	☐ Given to parents
☐ On file	☐ On file	☐ On file

Footprints/handprints
- ☐ Given to parents
- ☐ On file

ID bands/crib cards
- ☐ Given to parents
- ☐ On file

Lock of hair
- ☐ Given to parents
- ☐ On file

Mementos (clothing, hat, blanket)
- ☐ Given to parents
- ☐ On file

Complimentary birth certificate
- ☐ Given to parents
- ☐ On file

☐ Determine mother's discharge date as _____

☐ Inform about opportunity to postpone funeral until mother can attend

☐ Discuss options for services/funeral arrangements
- ☐ Self-transport
- ☐ Hospital chapel
- ☐ Graveside service
- ☐ Burial with a relative
- ☐ Specific area for babies in cemetery

Funeral arrangements by
- ☐ Mother
- ☐ Father

Discuss
- ☐ Seeing baby at funeral home
- ☐ Taking photos there
- ☐ Providing outfit/toy for baby

Give grief packet to
- ☐ Mother
- ☐ Father

Discuss grief process with
- ☐ Mother
- ☐ Father

Discuss grief conference with
- ☐ Mother
- ☐ Father

ONE-TO-ONE HELPER

☐ Plan grief conference with parents
Date _____
Time _____
Place _____
  ☐ Send confirmation letter

☐ Provide name/business card of one-to-one helper

☐ Send information on family to person keeping records of losses

☐ Offer information about parent support group
Date of first meeting attended _____
Follow-up meetings attended _____

☐ Offer option of another parent calling
  ☐ Accepted
  ☐ Declined
Parent contact _____

☐ Verify telephone number
  ☐ Learn optimal calling time

Follow-up calls
  ☐ One week
  ☐ Three weeks
  ☐ Due date
  ☐ Six to 10 months
  ☐ Anniversary date

PHYSICIAN

DEATH IN THE ANTEPARTUM SETTING
MISCARRIAGE, ECTOPIC PREGNANCY, STILLBIRTH

☐ Offer simple words of comfort; avoid cliches

☐ If named, use the baby's name

☐ Provide for privacy but do not leave the parents alone for long periods of time

☐ Offer comfortable seating

☐ Be sensitive to the needs of children if they are present

☐ Offer to call a support person

☐ Have someone make arrangements for transportation home

☐ Mention and discuss options
    ☐ Advantages/disadvantages of immediate medical intervention, such as dilatation and curettage or induction of labor
    ☐ Seeing baby or tissue
    ☐ Autopsy
    ☐ Genetic studies
    ☐ Blessing/baptism
    ☐ Memorial service/funeral

☐ Assess grief response; make sure parents receive appropriate reading material

☐ Discuss the following when and where appropriate
    ☐ Grief responses
    ☐ Incongruent grief
    ☐ Reaction of family and friends
    ☐ How to talk with children

☐ Offer ultrasound picture, if available

☐ Schedule next appointment during hours when gynecology, rather than obstetric, patients normally are seen

☐ See that a follow-up call or letter is sent to the parents one to two days after the loss if no immediate medical intervention is necessary

☐ Advise parents of your availability should they need to talk with you

Death During Hospitalization
Miscarriage, Ectopic Pregnancy, Stillbirth

Items on the following list are all important. However, consideration must be given to "timing."

☐ Offer simple words/gestures of comfort

Assess grief response of
- ☐ Mother
- ☐ Father
- ☐ Children

☐ Avoid uncomfortable silences

☐ Explain/discuss with father and mother all aspects of
- ☐ Miscarriage and dilatation and curettage
- ☐ Ectopic pregnancy and surgery
- ☐ Stillbirth and delivery

☐ Treat delivery of stillborn as a normal birth

☐ Make sure options are offered
- ☐ Seeing and holding baby
- ☐ Photographs
- ☐ Autopsy
- ☐ Genetic studies
- ☐ Blessing/baptism
- ☐ Memorial service
- ☐ Mementos

☐ Discuss sexuality after a loss

☐ Offer information concerning contraceptives

☐ Let parents have as much time as they wish with the baby

☐ Share your memories of the experience
- ☐ Concern for the mother and father
- ☐ The birth of the baby (if stillborn)
- ☐ If named, use the baby's name when talking to the parents
- ☐ Identify special characteristics of the baby

☐ Prescribe a medication to inhibit lactation

☐ Discuss physical and emotional responses after a loss
- ☐ Afterpains
- ☐ Lactation
- ☐ Aching arms
- ☐ Preoccupation with baby
- ☐ Incongruent grief
- ☐ Dreams
- ☐ Irritability
- ☐ Difficulty in concentration
- ☐ Moods

☐ Use touch and eye contact appropriately

☐ Mention grief conference

☐ Make sure follow-up appointment is during gynecology hours, if possible

☐ Advise parents of your availability should they need to talk with you

Newborn Death

- ☐ Use baby's name when talking about the baby

- ☐ Offer simple words/gestures of comfort

- ☐ Assess response of mother, father, grandparents, and children to anticipated newborn death
  - ☐ Chance for survival
  - ☐ Feelings of helplessness
  - ☐ Guilt
  - ☐ Hope
  - ☐ Bitterness
  - ☐ Withdrawal
  - ☐ Anxiety about surviving children

- ☐ Encourage visitation of other family members and friends

- ☐ Offer options when baby is clearly dying
  - ☐ Continue with full life support
  - ☐ Provide comfort measures, i.e., IVs, nutrition, and warmth
  - ☐ Take baby off all life support
  - ☐ Combination

- ☐ Explain about baby's pain; reassure them that the pain will be taken care of

- ☐ Explain what the parents might expect when the baby dies

- ☐ Facilitate time alone with the baby
  - ☐ Private setting
  - ☐ Baby to die in parents arms
  - ☐ Health care professional to be present
  - ☐ Holding baby
  - ☐ Let parents decide how much they want to be with baby

- ☐ Arrange for reverse transport of baby to mother's hospital, if applicable

- ☐ Follow up on options offered
  - ☐ Seeing and holding the baby
  - ☐ Photographs
  - ☐ Autopsy, if indicated
  - ☐ Genetic studies, if indicated
  - ☐ Baptism/blessing
  - ☐ Funeral/memorial service
  - ☐ Mementos

- ☐ Mention grief conference to be scheduled in four to six weeks

- ☐ Advise parents of your availability should they need to talk with you

- ☐ Call as soon as preliminary findings are completed

- ☐ Attend scheduled grief conference

PHYSICIAN

GRIEF CONFERENCE

☐ Review chart before conference

☐ If named, use the baby's name

☐ Explain the results of the autopsy and genetic studies

☐ Answer questions

☐ Do not press parents to talk if they do not want to; grief is private

☐ Assess the grief response of father, mother, and children to see how they are doing. Notice change in physical health.
   ☐ Sleeping patterns
   ☐ Changes in health status
   ☐ Social relationships
   ☐ Work experiences
   ☐ Guilt feelings

☐ Review normal grief response/process

☐ Share your memories of the experience
   ☐ Your thoughts and feelings at the time
   ☐ Special characteristics of the baby

☐ Recommend a physical examination four months after the loss

☐ Discuss risks of future pregnancies

☐ Identify studies which could be done in future pregnancies

☐ Advise parents of your availability should they need to talk with you

Do's And Don'ts For Physicians

DO

- Use eye contact and touch with families.
- Respond to families in a caring way, saying "I'm sorry."
- Use the baby's name or the word "baby."
- Treat miscarried and stillborn babies with respect.
- Treat the birth of a stillborn baby as you would a normal labor and delivery.
- Offer the family choices in making decisions.
- Allow parents to take care of their dying newborn.
- Allow families as much time as they need to say good-bye.
- Assess families for their grief responses.
- Emphasize the positive aspects of their baby and of their parenting.
- Make sure a baby is held as it is dying.
- Take into consideration your own feelings when a baby has died and find and use your own support system.

DON'T

- Assume a miscarriage is "just a miscarriage."
- Use cliches, such as "At least you can have others" or "There was probably something wrong with the baby anyway."
- Use words such as fetus, fetal wastage, remains, abortus, abortion, nonviable, defective in front of parents.
- Use forceps to pick up a baby.
- Place a stillborn baby in an instrument tray or metal basin after birth.
- Avoid looking families in the eye or talking with them about their decisions.
- Make decisions based on your values that could affect families' memories.

Funeral Director

For Assisting Parents Experiencing Miscarriage, Stillbirth, Or Newborn Death

☐ Visit with parents in hospital to discuss arrangements and role of the funeral director

☐ Involve both parents in planning when possible
  ☐ Mother　　　　　☐ Father　　　　☐ Both

☐ Encourage participation of other family/friends in services
  ☐ Grandparents　　☐ Children　　☐ Friends

☐ Discuss burial options
  ☐ Embalming
  ☐ Cremation
  ☐ Cemeteries
  ☐ Family plots
  ☐ Burial with a relative
  ☐ Burial in special area for babies in cemetery
  ☐ Casket options (parents to see what they look like open and closed)
  ☐ Opening the grave

☐ Discuss service/funeral options
  ☐ Role of funeral director in another state (if needed)
  ☐ Graveside
  ☐ Chapel
    ☐ Hospital　☐ Church
  ☐ Funeral home
  ☐ Private service
  ☐ Visitation
  ☐ Viewing of Baby
    ☐ Casket
      ☐ Open　☐ Closed　☐ Sealed
    ☐ Cradle
    ☐ Wicker Basket
    ☐ Other

☐ Discuss saying good-bye (for parents, family, and/or special friends)
  ☐ Private time
    ☐ Hold baby
    ☐ Dress or partially dress
    ☐ Wrap in blanket
    ☐ Rock baby
    ☐ Place baby in casket
  ☐ Special outfit for baby

Discuss saying good-bye (continued)

- ☐ Photographs
  - ☐ Funeral   ☐ Grave site   ☐ Baby in casket
- ☐ Write or help write
  - ☐ Obituary
  - ☐ Memorial folder for service
  - ☐ Eulogy
- ☐ Perform/participate in service
  - ☐ Parents   ☐ Family   ☐ Friends   ☐ Clergy
- ☐ Mementos to be placed with baby
  - ☐ Stuffed animal   ☐ Photographs
  - ☐ Toy   ☐ Handmade articles
  - ☐ Other _____
- ☐ Flowers
- ☐ Music
- ☐ Memorials
- ☐ Mementos for parents (if not already offered)
  - ☐ Lock of hair   ☐ Memorial card
  - ☐ Footprints   ☐ Photographs
  - ☐ Handprints   ☐ Copy of death certificate
  - ☐ Other _____
- ☐ Give grief information to
  - ☐ Mother   ☐ Grandparents
  - ☐ Father   ☐ Friends
  - Type of information
    - ☐ Books
    - ☐ Pamphlet
    - Title _____
- ☐ Discuss grief process with
  - ☐ Mother   ☐ Grandparents
  - ☐ Father   ☐ Friends
  - ☐ Children
- ☐ Provide cards or suggestions to help parents announce their baby's birth/death or express their appreciation for support
- ☐ Refer to appropriate grief support group or organization
- ☐ Give business card to
  - ☐ Mother
  - ☐ Father
- ☐ Follow-up call (two or three weeks later)

Comments:

_____

_____

_____

FUNERAL DIRECTOR

Clergy

For Assisting A Family Experiencing Miscarriage, Ectopic Pregnancy, Stillbirth Or Newborn Death

☐ Wear the hospital name tag given by the pastoral care department; introduce yourself to the physician, registered nurse, or other staff

☐ Be an advocate for the family by being certain they have been offered the following options
- ☐ Seeing and holding their baby
- ☐ Private time
- ☐ Family and friends present
- ☐ Photographs
- ☐ Mementos
- ☐ Funeral options
- ☐ Baptism/blessing
- ☐ Information on grief

☐ Make the baby an individual
- ☐ Call the baby by name
- ☐ Know the baby's sex when possible
- ☐ Touch the baby
- ☐ Ask to see photographs
- ☐ Comment on the baby's characteristics

☐ If a member of a hospital pastoral care department, share information with family's own clergy

☐ Make baptism special, even if it occurs quickly and in a hospital setting
- ☐ Include family and friends
- ☐ Save mementos
- ☐ Talk with primary nurse beforehand to ask what special characteristics the parents have noticed
- ☐ Use a sea shell for baptism and give it to the family
- ☐ Hand carry the baptismal certificate with a letter to the parents

☐ Talk with siblings, grandparents, and other close relatives and friends

☐ Offer books, pamphlets, a bibliography, and other resources on grief

☐ Give parents information on various types of services
- ☐ Memorial service
- ☐ Funeral
- ☐ Graveside service
- ☐ Commemorative service (on an anniversary date, or many years after the loss)
- ☐ Hospital chapel

☐ Assist the parents with a service
   ☐ Go over the total service
   ☐ Invite them to choose the Bible verses
   ☐ Invite them to write all or part of the service
   ☐ Invite them to write something for the service which can be placed in the casket
   ☐ Make the sermon or eulogy personal by talking about the baby (the teddy bear in the baby's isolette, a song the mom sang during the baby's last hour, what the baby was wrapped in, etc.), the pregnancy (when the parents told you they were pregnant), and special plans the parents had for the baby
   ☐ Include siblings in the service if the parents and children wish
   ☐ Tape record the service if the parents wish

☐ Call in the family a week after discharge from the hospital, then a month, six months, and a year later.

☐ Mobilize support in their church by sharing reading material on perinatal grief with members of the congregation. Think of another couple who has had a similar loss you might introduce to the family later on.

☐ Mention the baby and family in "Prayers for the People" or "Pastoral Prayer," but only with the permission of the family

CLERGY

BIBLIOGRAPHY

PREGNANCY, PARENTING, AND BONDING

Clark, A.L., & Affonso, D.D. (1979). *Childbearing: A nursing perspective.* (2nd ed.). Philadelphia: Davis Co.

Clark, A.L., & Affonso, D.D. (1976). Infant behavior and maternal attachment: Two sides to the coin. *American Journal of Maternal Child Nursing, 1,* 93-99.

Fischman, S.H., et al. (1986). Changes in sexual relationships in postpartum couples. *Journal of Obstetric, Gynecologic, and Neonatal Nursing, 15,* 58-63.

Galinsky, E. (1981). *Between generations: The six stages of parenthood.* New York: Times Books.

Klaus, M.H., & Kennell, J.H. (1982). *Parent-infant bonding* (2nd ed.). St. Louis: The C.V. Mosby Company.

Lederman, R. (1984). *Psychosocial adaptation in pregnancy.* Englewood Cliffs, N.J.: Prentice Hall, Inc.

GRIEF

Berezin, N. (1982). *After a loss in pregnancy.* New York: Simon and Schuster.

Berg, B. (1981). *Nothing to cry about.* New York: Seaview Books.

Borg, S., & Lasker, J. (1981). *When pregnancy fails.* Boston: Beacon Press.

Bowlby, J., & Parkes, C.M. (1970). Separation and loss within the family. In E.J. Anthony & C. Koupernik (Eds.), *The child in his family.* New York: Wiley.

Carr, D., & Knupp, Chaplain S. (1985). Grief and perinatal loss: A community hospital approach to support. *Journal of Obstetric, Gynecologic, and Neonatal Nursing, 14* (2), 130-139.

Chez, R. (moderator). (1982). Helping patients and doctors cope with perinatal death. *Contemporary Ob/Gyn, 20,* 98+.

Ciaramitaro, B. (1982). *Help for depressed mothers.* Edmonds, WA: The Chas. Franklin Press.

Coffin, W.S. Jr. (1984, April 20). My son beat me to the grave. *The Lutheran Standard,* pp. 4-7.

Davidson, G.W. (1979). *Understanding death of the wished for child.* Springfield, IL: OGR Service Corp. (P.O. Box 3586, Springfield, IL 62708).

Davidson, G.W. (1984). *Understanding mourning*. Minneapolis: Augsburg Publishing House.

Ewy, D., & Ewy, R. (1984). *Death of a dream: Miscarriage, stillbirth and newborn loss*. New York: E.P. Dutton, Inc.

Friedman, R., & Gradstein, B. (1982). *Surviving pregnancy loss*. Boston: Little Brown Co.

Genesis (entire issue). (1982, June/July), *4* (3).

Grief related to perinatal death. (1985). (Tech. Bul. No. 13). Washington, DC: NAACOG.

Grollman, E. (1981). *What helped me when my loved one died*. Boston: Beacon Press.

Grove, S., et al. (1978). Encounters with grief. *American Journal of Nursing, 78*, 414-425.

Ilse, S. (1982). *Empty arms: Coping with miscarriage, stillbirth and infant death*. Long Lake, MN: Wintergreen Press. (4105 Oak St., Long Lake, MN 55356).

Jackson, P.L. (1985). When the baby isn't perfect.*American Journal of Nursing, 85* (4), 396-399.

Kowalski, K. (1984). *Perinatal death: An ethnomethodological study of factors influencing perinatal bereavement*. Unpublished doctoral dissertation, University of Colorado, Boulder, CO.

Limbo, R.K., & Wheeler, S.R. (1986). Coping with unexpected outcomes. *NAACOG Update Series, 5* (3), 1-8.

Limbo, R.K., & Wheeler, S.R. (1985). Family-centered care for bereaved families. *The Cybele Report, 6* (3), 3-6.

Manning, D. (1985). *Comforting those who grieve: A guide for helping others*. San Francisco: Harper and Row.

Manning, D. (1984). *Don't take my grief away from me*. San Francisco: Harper and Row for Insight Books.

Panuthos, C., & Romeo, C. (1984). *Ended beginnings: Healing childbearing losses*. Hadley, MA: Bergin & Garvey Publishers, Inc.

Peppers, L.G., & Knapp, R. (1985). *How to go on living after the death of a baby*. Atlanta, GA: Peachtree Publishers, Ltd.

Peppers, L.G., & Knapp, R. (1980). *Motherhood and mourning*. New York: Praeger Publishers.

Poznanski, E.O. (1972). The "replacement child": A saga of unresolved parental grief. *Journal of Pediatrics, 81*, 1190-1193.

Rando, T. (1984). *Grief, dying and death.* Champaign, IL: Research Press Company.

Resolve Through Sharing. (1984) *It means so much to know that someone cares.* La Crosse, WI: La Crosse Lutheran Hospital.

Rowe, J., et al. (1978). Follow-up of families who experience a perinatal death. *Pediatrics, 62,* 166-170.

Schiff, H. (1977). *The bereaved parent.* New York: Crown Publishers.

Schodt, C. (1982, February/March). Grief in adolescent mothers after an infant death. *Image.* pp. 20-25.

Schwiebert, P., & Kirk, P. (1981, 1985). *When hello means goodbye.* Portland, OR: Perinatal Loss.

Stearns, A.K. (1984). *Living through personal crisis.* Chicago: Thomas More Press.

Westberg, G. (1971). *Good grief.* Philadelphia: Fortress Press.

Wong, D.L. (1980). Bereavement: The empty-mother syndrome. *American Journal of Maternal Child Nursing, 5,* 384-389.

York, C.R., & Stichler, J. (1985). Cultural grief expressions following infant death. *Dimensions of Critical Care Nursing, 4* (2), 120-127.

Zahourek, R., & Jensen, J.S. (1973). Grieving and the loss of the newborn. *American Journal of Nursing, 78,* 836-839.

MISCARRIAGE/ECTOPIC PREGNANCY

Ilse, S., & Burns, L.H. (1985). *Miscarriage . . . A shattered dream.* Long Lake, MN: Wintergreen Press. (4105 Oak St., Long Lake, MN 55356).

Johnson, J., et al. (1983). *Miscarriage.* Omaha: Centering Corporation.

Kuczynski, H.J. (1986, July/August). Support for the woman with an ectopic pregnancy. *Journal of Obstetric, Gynecologic, and Neonatal Nursing, 15* (4), 306-309.

Merrill, S.E. (1986). *Miscarriage and the fathers: The need for and availability of social support.* Unpublished master's thesis, University of Wisconsin - Eau Claire School of Nursing, Eau Claire, WI.

Moghissi, K. (1982). What causes habitual abortion? *Contemporary Ob/Gyn, 20,* 45-60, 64.

Phillips, S.G. (1980, July). Coping with miscarriage . . . my own experience. *American Baby,* pp. 38-39.

Pizer, H., & Palinski, C. (1981). *Coping with a miscarriage.* New York: New American Library.

Pizer, H., & Palinski, C. (1981, September). Coping with a miscarriage. *American Baby*, p. 42+.

Stephany, T. (1982). Early miscarriage: Are we too quick to dismiss the pain? *RN, 45*, 89.

Swanson-Kauffman, K.M. (1986). Caring in the instance of unexpected early pregnancy loss. *Topics in Clinical Nursing, 8* (2), 37-46.

Wall-Haas, C.L. (1985). Women's perceptions of first trimester spontaneous abortion. *Journal of Obstetric, Gynecologic, and Neonatal Nursing, 14* (1), 50-53.

Wetzel, S.K. (1982). Are we ignoring the needs of the woman with a spontaneous abortion? *American Journal of Maternal Child Nursing, 7*, 258-259.

STILLBIRTH

Beard, R.K., et al. (1978). Help for parents after stillbirth. *British Medical Journal, 1*, 172-173.

Breuer, J. (1976). Sharing a tragedy. *American Journal of Nursing, 76*, 758-759.

Bruce, S. (1962). Reactions of nurses and mothers to stillborns. *Nursing Outlook, 10*, 88+.

Crout, T.K. (1980). Caring for the mother of a stillborn baby. *Nursing '80, 10*, 70-73.

Kirkley-Best, E., & Kellner, K. (1982). The forgotten grief: Review of the psychology of stillbirth. *American Journal of Orthopsychiatry, 52* (3), 400-429.

Kish, G. (1978). Note on C. Grubb's body image concerns of a multipara in the situation of intrauterine fetal death. *American Journal of Maternal Child Nursing, 7*, 111.

Kowalski, K., et al. (1977). Helping mothers of stillborn infants to grieve. *American Journal of Maternal Child Nursing, 2*, 29.

Kowalski, K. (1980). Managing perinatal loss. *Clinical Ob/Gyn, 23*, 1113-1123.

Kowalski, K., & Bowes, W., M.D. (1976). Parents' response to a stillborn baby. *Contemporary Ob/Gyn, 16*, 53-57.

Lewis, E. (1979). Mourning by the family after a stillbirth or neonatal death. *Archives of Disease in Childhood, 54*, 303-306.

Moriarity, D. (1982, November). The right to mourn. *Ms. Magazine*, pp. 79-81.

Saylor, Rev. D.E. (1977). Nursing response to mothers of stillborn infants. *Journal of Obstetric and Gynecologic Nursing, 6,* 39-42.

NEWBORN DEATH

Clyman, D.I., et al. (1980). Issues concerning parents after the death of their newborn. *Critical Care Medicine, 8,* 215-218.

Courtney, S.E., Thomas, N., & Predmore, B.K. (1985). Reverse transport of the deceased neonate - an aid to mourning. *American Journal of Perinatology, 2* (3), 217-220.

Elliott, B.A., & Hein, H.H. (1978). Neonatal death: Reflections for physicians. *Pediatrics, 62,* 96-99.

Elliott, B.A. (1978). Neonatal death: Reflections for parents. *Pediatrics, 62,* 100-102.

Hagan, J.M. (1974). Infant death - nursing interaction and intervention with grieving families. *Nursing Forum, 3,* 373-385.

Stinson, R., & Stinson, P. (1983). *The long dying of baby Andrew.* Boston: Little, Brown and Company.

SIBLING RESPONSE

Arnold, J.H., & Gemma, P.B. (1983). *A child dies: A portrait of family grief.* Rockville, MD: Aspen Systems Corporation.

Dodge, N., & Lamb, Sr. J.M. (1985). *Sharing with Thumpy* (workbook). Springfield, IL: Prairie Lark Press. (P.O. Box 699, Springfield, IL 62705).

Dodge, N. (1983). *Thumpy's story.* Springfield, IL: Prairie Lark Press. (P.O. Box 699, Springfield, IL 62705).

Dodge, N., & Lamb, Sr. J.M. (1985). *Thumpy's story - A story to color.* Springfield, IL: Prairie Lark Press. (P.O. Box 699, Springfield, IL 62705).

Grollman, E.A. (Ed.). (1967). *Explaining death to children.* Boston: Beacon Press.

Grollman, E.A. (1976). *Talking about death: A dialogue between parent and child.* Boston: Beacon Press.

Jackson, E.N. (1965). *Telling a child about death.* New York: Channel Press.

Jewett, C. (1982). *Helping children cope with separation and loss.* Harvard, MA: Harvard Common Press.

Koch, J. (1977, November). When children meet death. *Psychology Today.* pp. 64-66.

Krell, R., & Rabkin, L. (1970). The effects of sibling death on the surviving child: A family perspective. *Family Process, 18*, 471-477.

Mellonie, B., & Ingpen, R. (1983). *Lifetimes.* New York: Bantam Books, Inc.

Mills, G.C. (1979). Books to help children understand death. *American Journal of Nursing, 79*, 291-295.

O'Connor, K. (1980). How to talk to your child about death. *Liguorian, 68*, 34-38.

Oehler, J. (1978). *The frog family's baby dies* (coloring book). Durham, NC: Duke University Medical Center.

Sahler, O.J.Z. (1978). *The child and death.* St. Louis: The C.V. Mosby Company.

Schaefer, D., & Lyons, C. (1986). *How do we tell the children?* New York: Newmarket Press.

Scrimshaw, S.C.M., & March, D.M.S. (1984, Feb. 10). 'I had a baby sister but she only lasted one day.' *Journal of the American Medical Association, 251* (6), 732-733.

Viorst, J. (1971). *The tenth good thing about Barney.* New York: Atheneum Publishers.

SELF-HELP GROUPS

Braun, L., Coplon, J., & Sonnenschein, P. (1984) *Helping parents in groups: A leader's handbook.* Boston: Resource Communications, Inc.

Prindle, P., & Williams, R.T. (1981). *Self-help/mutual support groups: Principles and practices for the helping professional.* (Available from University of Wisconsin Extension, Madison, WI)

GRIEF COUNSELING

Black, Sr. Kathleen. (1983). *Short-term counseling.* Menlo Park, CA: Addison-Wesley Publishing Co., Inc.

Rauen, K. (1985). The telephone as stethoscope. *American Journal of Maternal Child Nursing, 10*, 122-124.

Worden, J.W. (1982). *Grief counseling and grief therapy.* New York: Springer Publishing Company, Inc.

PICTURE TAKING

Johnson, J., et al. (1985). *A most important picture.* Omaha: Centering Corporation. (P.O. Box 3367, Omaha, NE 68103-0367).

ADDITIONAL SUPPORT MATERIALS

PARENTS' INFORMATION

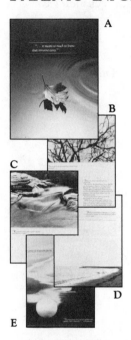

A Parents' Booklet - includes folder cover (**RTS 4111**) and 32 page insert explaining the grief process, loss of a future, saying good-bye, explaining death to children and other adults, planning another pregnancy, & sexuality. The pockets are designed to accept pertinent materials regarding ectopic pregnancy, miscarriage & autopsy.
RTS 4112 .... **$4.25 for one**

B Miscarriage - a six page brochure addressing both emotional and physical responses to a miscarriage. Discusses feelings of both men and women. **RTS 4113** .... **$.75 for one**

C Autopsy - a two page flyer explaining what an autopsy is. Discusses things for parents to think about in making this decision. **RTS 4114** .... **$.26 for one**

D Ectopic Pregnancy - this four page brochure discusses responses to ectopic pregnancy. Included are diagrams showing possible sites for implantation. **RTS 4115**...... **$.51 for one**

E The Grief of Grandparents - this eight page booklet provides an enlightening look at the feelings of grandparents. Gives practical advice on how to help. The back page has a Remembrance of Blessing prayer and allows Keepsake space to record information about their grandchild.
RTS 4116 .... **$1.31 for one**

HEALTH CARE MATERIALS

F Door Cards - 4¼ x 6¼ four-color card to be placed on the hospital room door of the bereaved parents to indicate their loss. **RTS 6101** .... **$ 1.25 for five**

G Parents' Introduction Brochure - An introduction to the one-to-one counseling program and follow-up support. Each brochure is printed especially with hospital name, phone number and individual information and dates of follow-up program. Allow 3 weeks for printing from receipt of information and order. The Lutheran Hospital/Gundersen Clinic, Ltd. sample is available upon request.
RTS 4101.......................... **$95.20 for 100**

H Parents' Folder - 9 x 11 four-color folder with pockets in front and rear designed to hold the *Resolve Through Sharing* Counselor Card and other literature. **RTS 4111**...... **$ 9.90 for five**

I *Resolve Through Sharing Tear Drop Lapel Pin* - in white and blue on gold-colored metal, 3/8" in diameter.... **$ 3.00 each**

COMPLETE SAMPLE RTS KIT - one each of 32 page Parents' Booklet, Miscarriage, Ectopic, Grandparents, Autopsy, "Remembrance of Blessing," "In Memory Of," Parents' Introduction Brochure, Door Card, and sample stationery. Reflects 10% discount **$8.70**

PROPORTIONAL PACKAGES of Miscarriage, Autopsy, Ectopic, and The Grief of Grandparents, based on annual births:

MD Offices or Basic Proportional Package - includes 5 Miscarriage, 1 Ectopic, 3 Grandparents, and 1 Autopsy. Reflects a 5% discount from single purchase of individual pieces **$8.02**

Hospital I - based on 356 deliveries annually. Includes 25 Miscarriage, 5 Ectopic, 15 Grandparents, and 3 Autopsy. Reflects a 15% discount from single purchase of individual pieces............................... **$35.47**

Hospital II - based on 600 deliveries annually. Includes 50 Miscarriage, 10 Ectopic, 30 Grandparents, and 5 Autopsy. Reflects a 20% discount from single purchase of individual pieces............................... **$66.56**

Hospital III - based on 1400 deliveries annually. Includes 100 Miscarriage, 20 Ectopic, 60 Grandparents, 20 Autopsy. Reflects 25% discount from single purchase of individual pieces **$126.75**

HEALTH CARE PROGRAMS/PROGRAM MATERIALS

3-day Counselor Certification Course

Three-day counselor certification is designed to provide participants with the skills they need in responding to families who have lost a baby through miscarriage, stillbirth, and newborn death. Intended for nurses, social workers, clergy, physicians, and funeral directors, the course explores emotional, physical, spiritual and legal issues which affect the bereavement process. **Registration fee is $225 which includes lunches, breaks & a *Resolve Through Sharing* counselor's manual.**

One-day Hospital Coordinator Certification

Hospital Coordinator Certification is intended for professionals who are: already *Resolve Through Sharing* Counselors OR will become a *Resolve Through Sharing* Counselor prior to Coordinator Certification.

A *Resolve Through Sharing* Hospital Coordinator heads the *Resolve Through Sharing* comprehensive program. This program ensures that consistent, sensitive care is given to each and every grieving parent and family from the moment the baby is lost, through the period of grieving and for as long as the family desires.

Resolve Through Sharing Hospital Coordinators are able to educate other professionals in their hospital and its service area, as *Resolve Through Sharing* counselors. The hospital a coordinator represents is able to call itself a *Resolve Through Sharing* Hospital. The hospital coordinator is responsible for filing an annual report with *Resolve Through Sharing* headquarters. Counselors educated by the hospital coordinator are each required to have their own counselor manual. **Registration fee is $325, which includes (2) hospital program manuals, (1) coordinator manual, lunch, breaks and a dinner.**

Hospital Sponsorship of a *Resolve Through Sharing* 3-day Counselor Certification Course

Hospitals that sponsor a 3-day counselor certification course have the cost-effective opportunity to have professionals from their hospital certified as *Resolve Through Sharing* counselors by the *Resolve Through Sharing* National Director & Director of Education. In addition the sponsoring hospital receives the following ($880 value) at no charge: (2) Resolve Through Sharing *Program Development Manuals*; 24 Parents' Kits which include: A Door Card, an

"In Memory Of" Card, a Remembrance of Blessing, and a Parents' Booklet; Unlimited Phone Consultation for the Resolve Through Sharing *Coordinator with RTS/LLH; Community Education Program (2-hour) designed to build community awareness; One-Day Hospital Coordinator Certification.* **The sponsoring hospital is free to charge tuition and it is recommended a fee of $225 be charged/participant.**

Hospital Program Manuals

The *Resolve Through Sharing* comprehensive hospital program and development manual can assist your staff and hospital in providing consistent, sensitive care. Each and every grieving parent and family who experiences the loss of a baby through miscarriage, ectopic pregnancy, stillbirth or newborn death can be reached. The *Resolve Through Sharing* hospital manual provides protocols, guidelines, and checklists. These enable hospital staff to provide supportive care to parents from the moment a baby is lost, through the period of grieving and for as long as the family desires.

The hospital program manual includes sections on: *Hospital Self-Inventory; Writing Program Objectives; Setting Up a Planning Committee; Planning Committee Tasks; Interviewing & Selecting* Resolve Through Sharing *Counselors;* Resolve Through Sharing *Coordinator & Counselor Roles; Policies, Protocols, Guidelines, & Checklists for implementing* Resolve Through Sharing; *How to Start a Parent Support Group; Guidelines on Promoting Awareness; Suggestions for Inservice Education; Bibliography.* **Two hospital manuals ($200); One hospital manual ($175)**

One-day Sensitivity Workshop

One-day workshops are available to hospitals, groups and communities. These presentations create an awareness of the grieving process and the impact of miscarriage, ectopic pregnancy, stillbirth, and newborn death on parents.

FUNERAL DIRECTOR/CLERGY MATERIALS

J **"In Memory Of"** - 8½ x 11 Keepsake Record printed in four-color for parents. Includes blanks to record information about the baby and space for footprints and photos. **RTS 6111** .... **$ 3.95 for five**

K **"Remembrance of Blessing"** - 5½ x 8½ four-color card which includes a Blessing for the baby, and space for information about the baby, the date, and the administrator of the Blessing. **RTS 6121** .... **$ 1.80 for five**

L **"Gone But Not Forgotten"** - Sympathy Cards with envelopes .... **$ 3.60 for five**

See Support Material for Parents

M **The Grief of Grandparents** - this eight page booklet provides an enlightening look at the feelings of grandparents. Gives practical advice on how to help. The back page has a Remembrance of Blessing prayer and allows Keepsake space to record information about their grandchild. **RTS 4116** .... **$1.31 for one**

N **Parents' Booklet** - includes folder cover (**RTS 4111**) and 32 page insert explaining the grief process, loss of a future, saying good-bye, explaining death to children and other adults, planning another pregnancy, & sexuality. The pockets are designed to accept pertinent materials regarding ectopic pregnancy, miscarriage & autopsy. **RTS 4112** .... **$4.25 for one**

This ordering page is provided for your convenience and may be copied.

Please send _____ copies of *When A Baby Dies* for $8.95 each. $ _____

5% WI Sales Tax $ _____

Add $2.00 per book $ _____
for shipping and handling.
For large quantities,
shipping will be billed.

Total $ _____

Make checks payable to, and mail order to, *Resolve Through Sharing*
La Crosse Lutheran Hospital
1910 South Avenue
La Crosse, WI 54601

Ordered By: _____

Send To: _____

Address: _____

Telephone: _____